Sue & Tai-chan

Konami Kanata

Contents

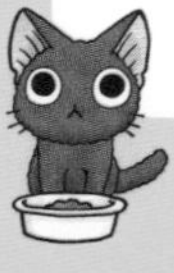

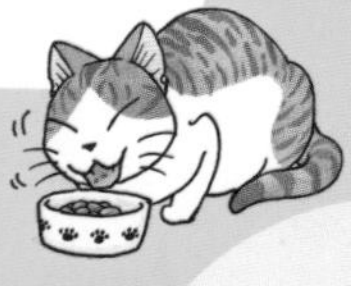

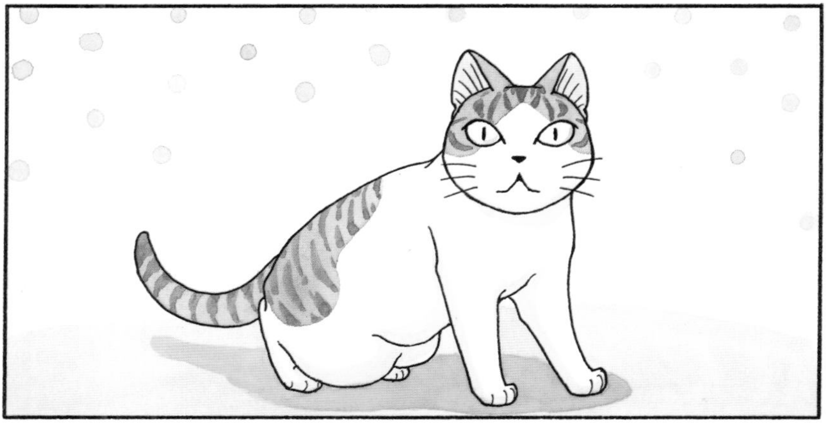

CHAPTER 1 Here's Tai-chan!

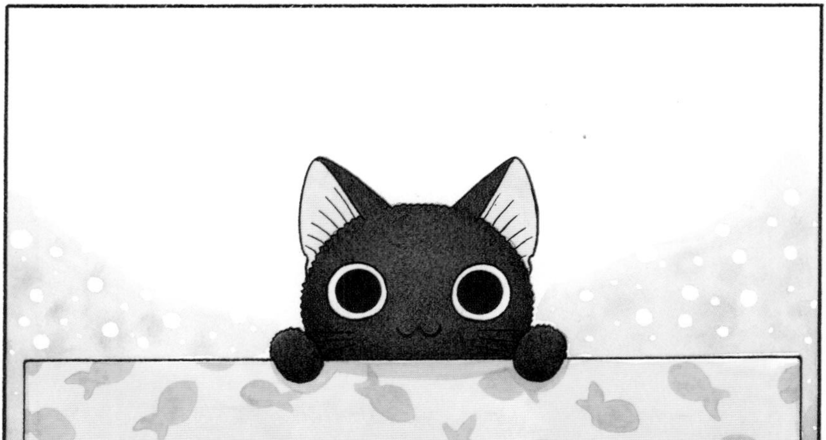

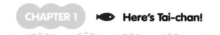

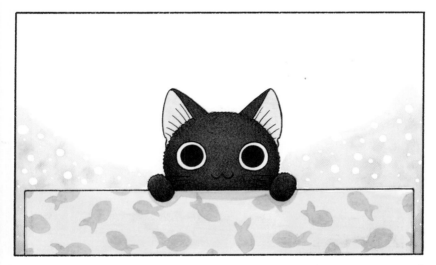

Sue & Tai-chan

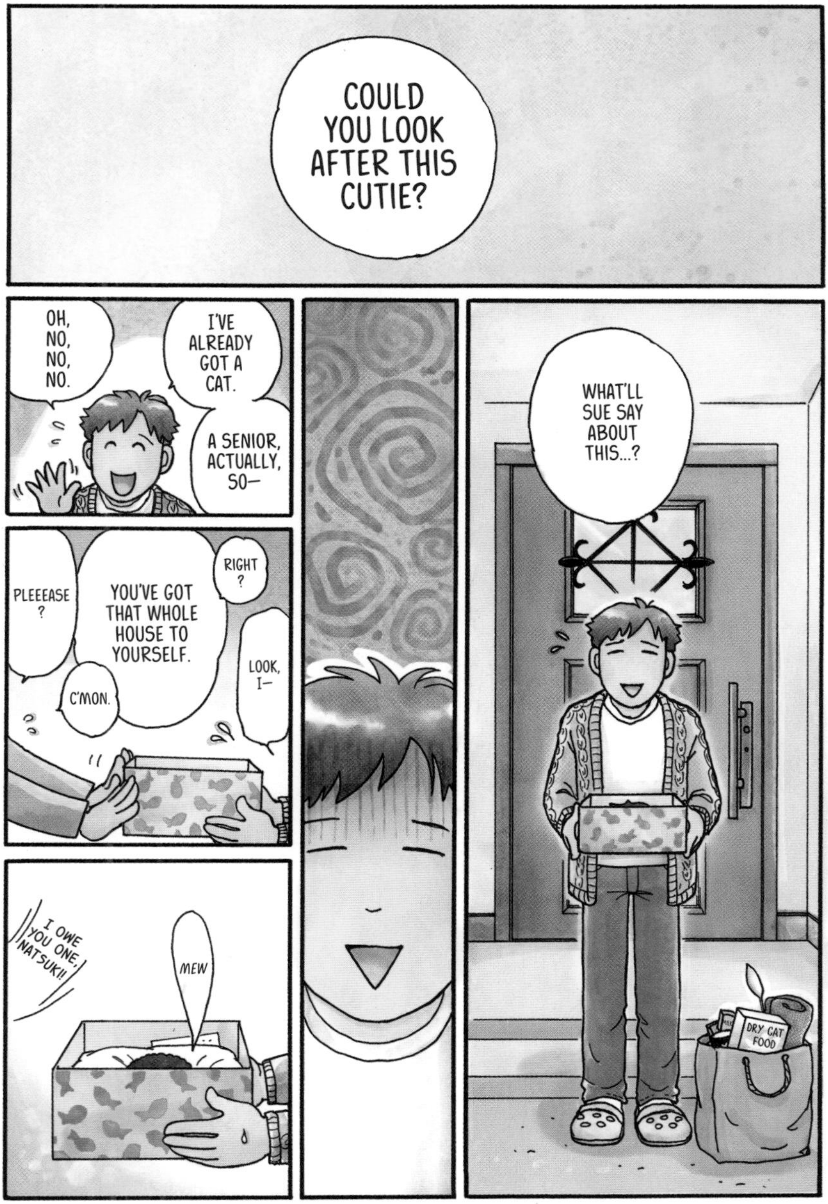
COULD YOU LOOK AFTER THIS CUTIE?
OH, NO, NO, NO.
I'VE ALREADY GOT A CAT.
A SENIOR, ACTUALLY, SO—
PLEEEASE?
YOU'VE GOT THAT WHOLE HOUSE TO YOURSELF.
RIGHT?
C'MON.
LOOK, I—
I OWE YOU ONE, NATSUK!!
MEW
WHAT'LL SUE SAY ABOUT THIS...?
DRY CAT FOOD

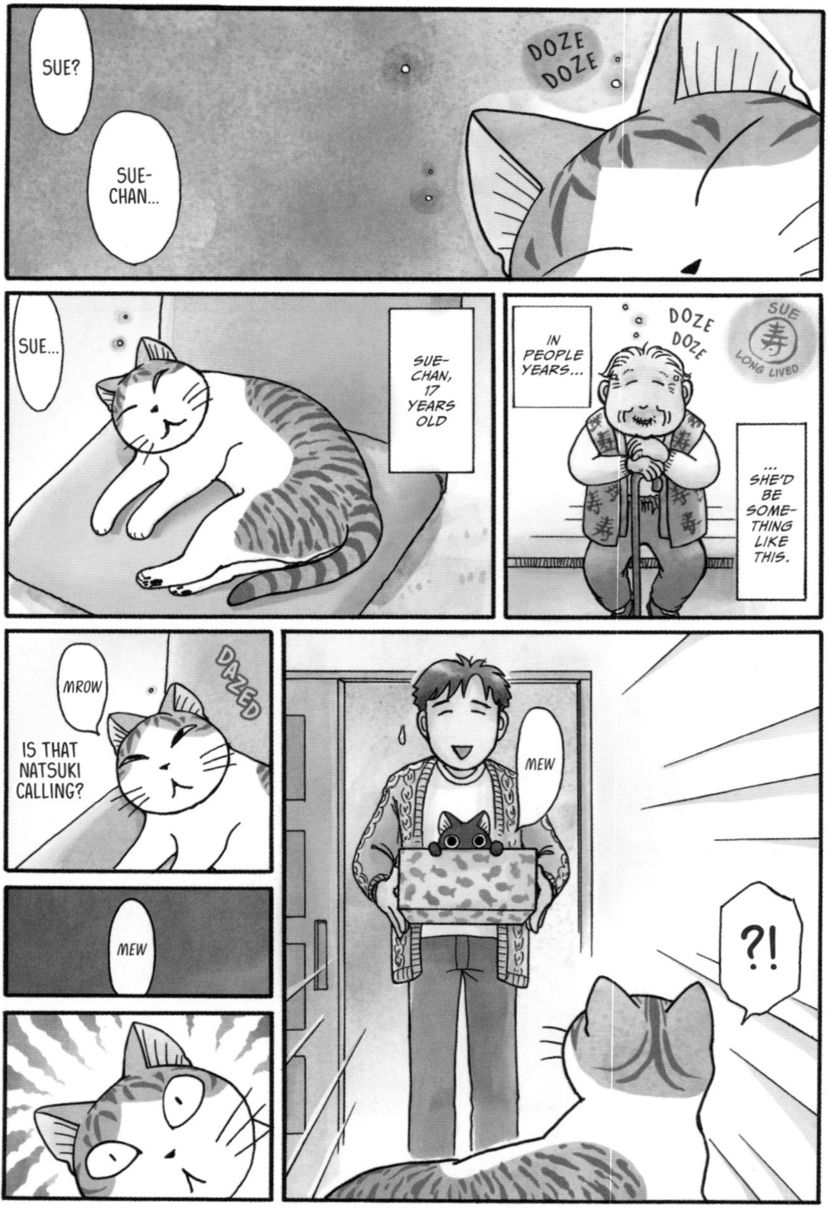
SUE?
SUE-CHAN...
DOZE DOZE
SUE...
SUE-CHAN, 17 YEARS OLD
IN PEOPLE YEARS...
DOZE DOZE
SUE
寿
LONG LIVED
...SHE'D BE SOME-THING LIKE THIS.
MROW
DAZED
IS THAT NATSUKI CALLING?
MEW
MEW
?!

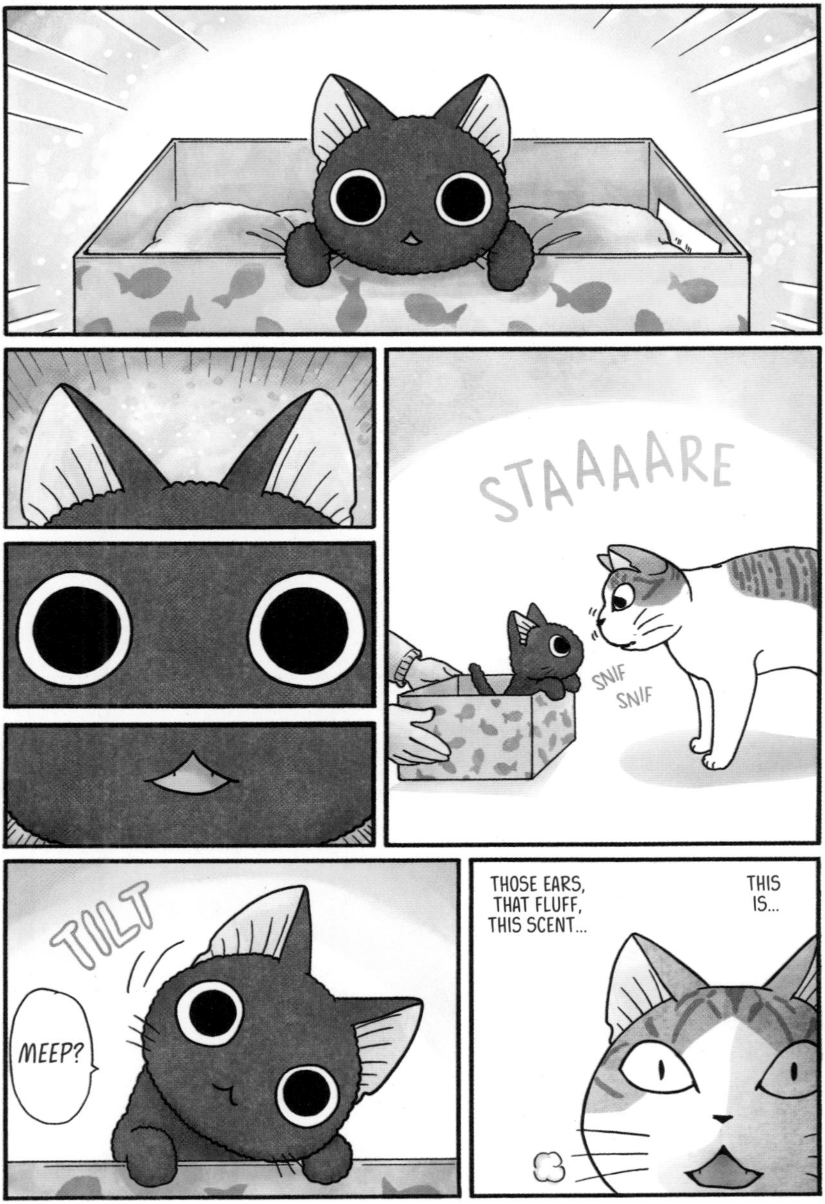
STAAAARE
SNIF SNIF
TILT
MEEP?
THOSE EARS, THAT FLUFF, THIS SCENT...
THIS IS...

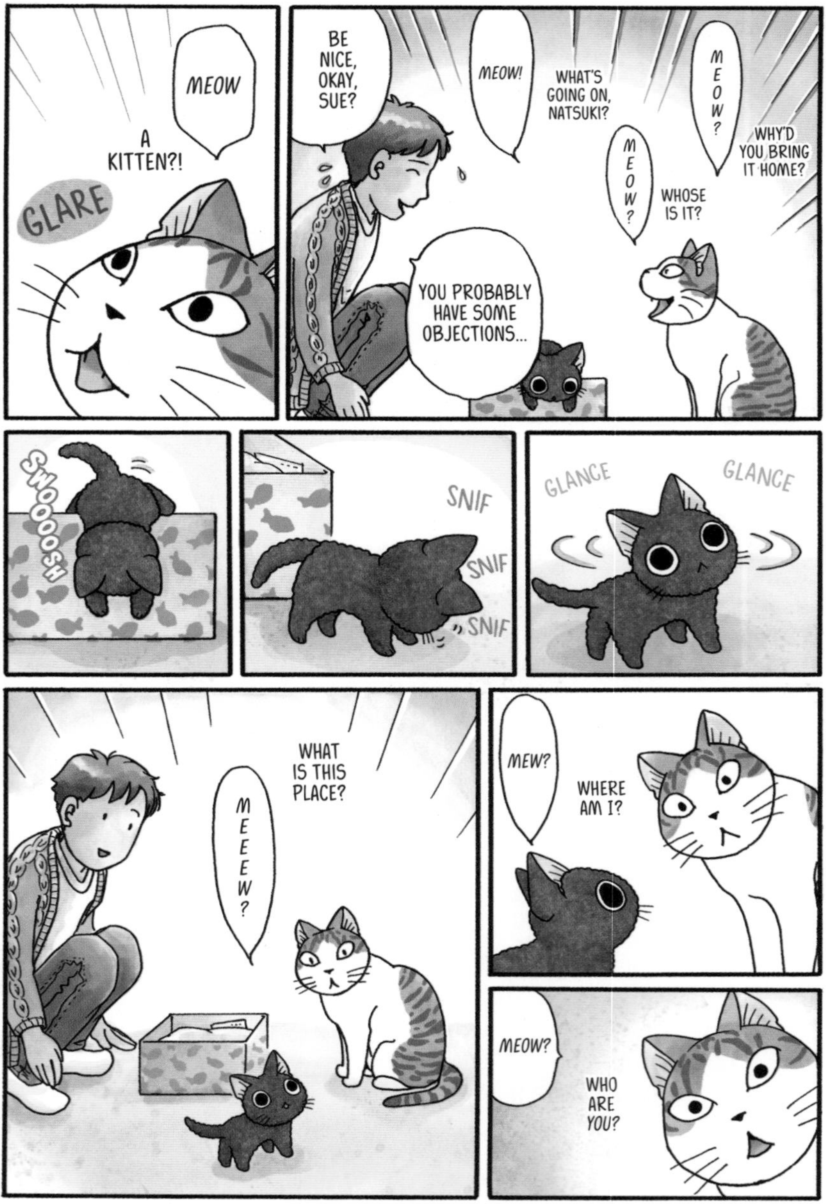
MEOW
A KITTEN?!
GLARE
BE NICE, OKAY, SUE?
MEOW!
WHAT'S GOING ON, NATSUKI?
MEOW?
WHY'D YOU BRING IT HOME?
MEOW?
WHOSE IS IT?
YOU PROBABLY HAVE SOME OBJECTIONS...
SWOOOOSH
SNIF
SNIF
SNIF
GLANCE
GLANCE
WHAT IS THIS PLACE?
MEEEEW?
MEW?
WHERE AM I?
MEOW?
WHO ARE YOU?

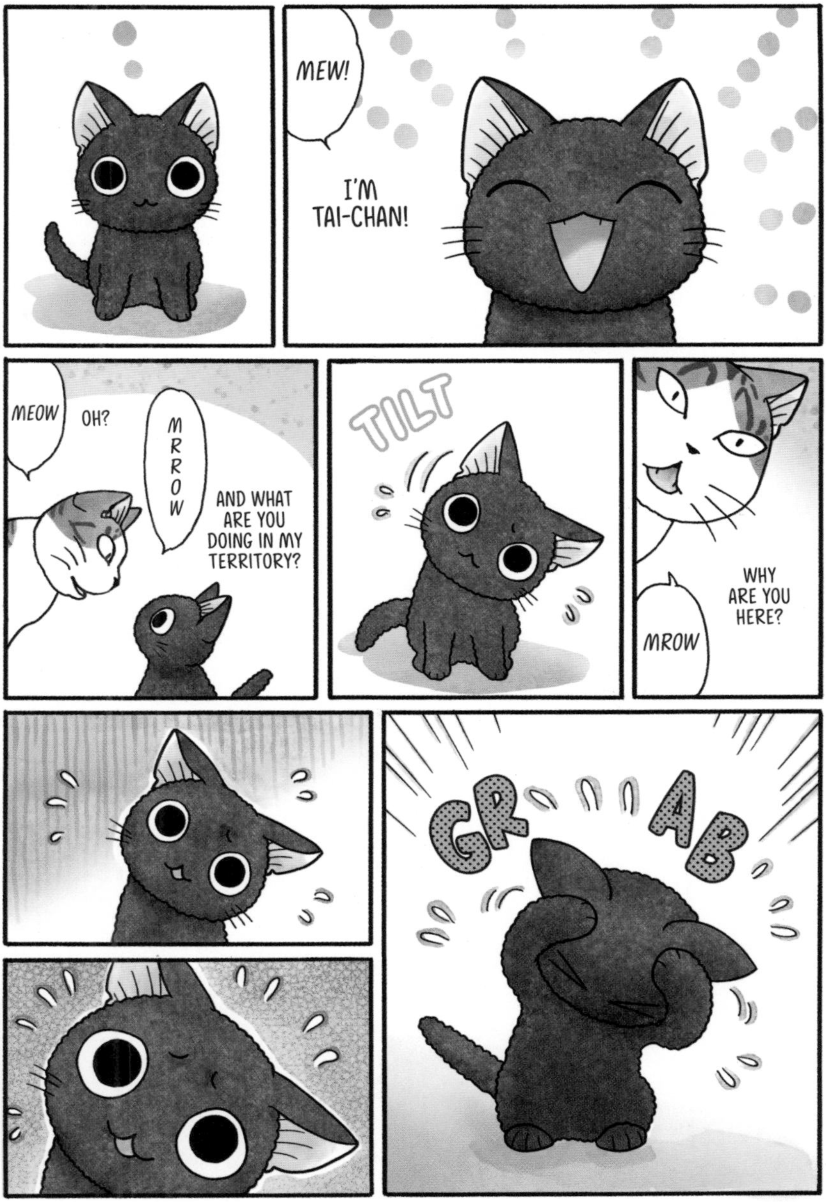
MEW!
I'M TAI-CHAN!
MEOW
OH?
MRROW
AND WHAT ARE YOU DOING IN MY TERRITORY?
TILT
WHY ARE YOU HERE?
MROW
GRAB

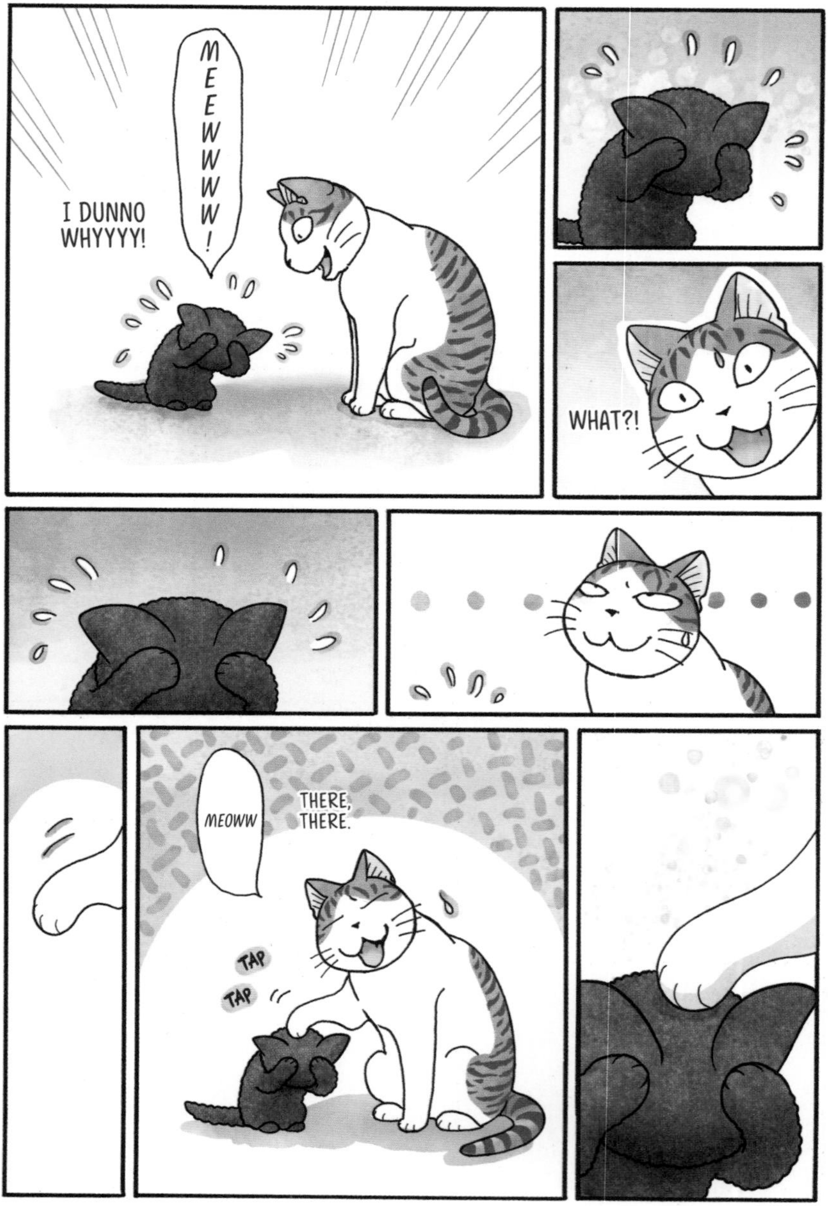
I DUNNO WHYYYY!
MEEWWWWW!
WHAT?!
MEOWW
THERE, THERE.
TAP
TAP

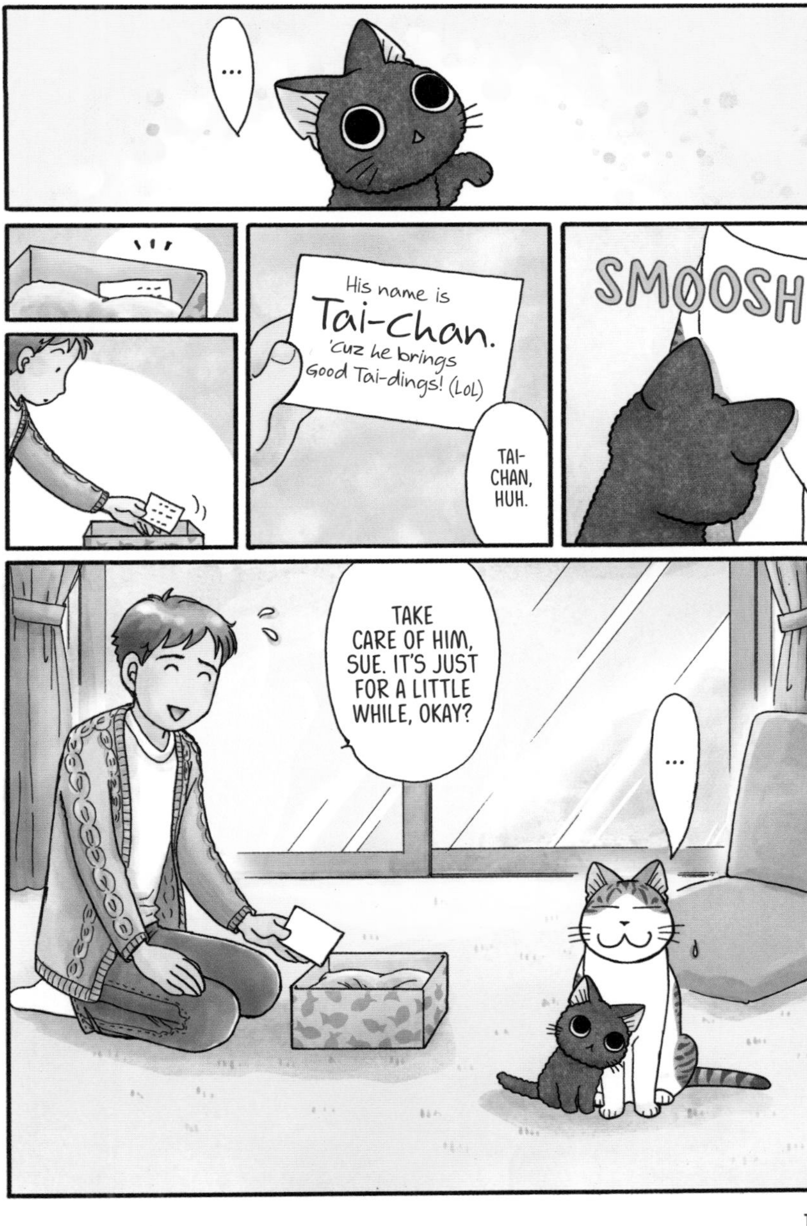
...
His name is Tai-Chan. 'Cuz he brings Good Tai-dings! (LOL)
TAI-CHAN, HUH.
SMOOSH
TAKE CARE OF HIM, SUE. IT'S JUST FOR A LITTLE WHILE, OKAY?
...

Sue & Tai-chan

CHAPTER 2 Beginning of the Two-Cat Lifestyle

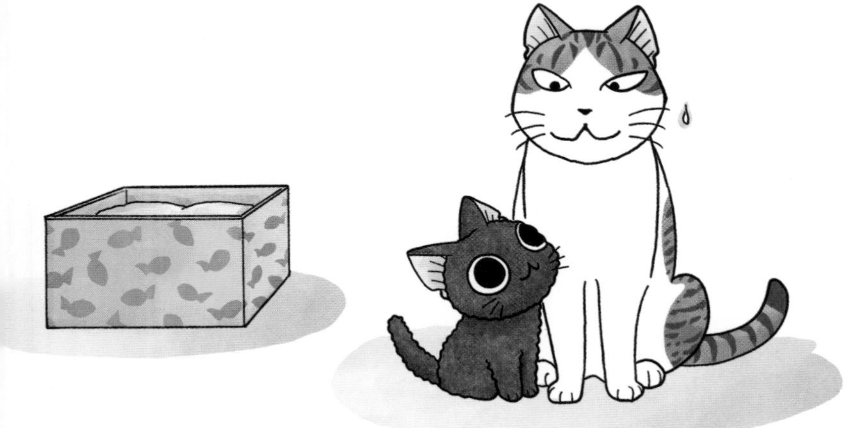

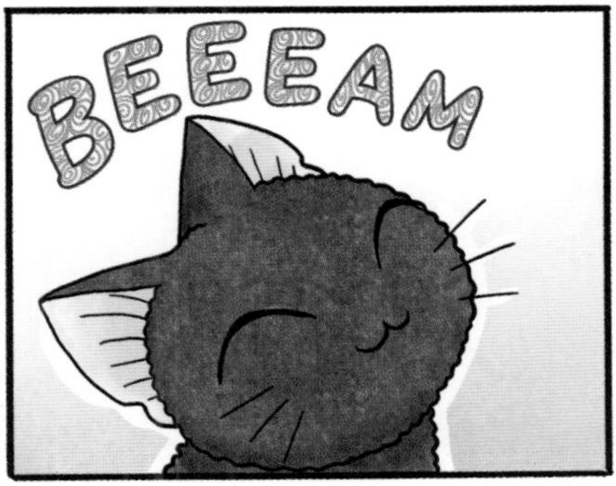
BEEEAM

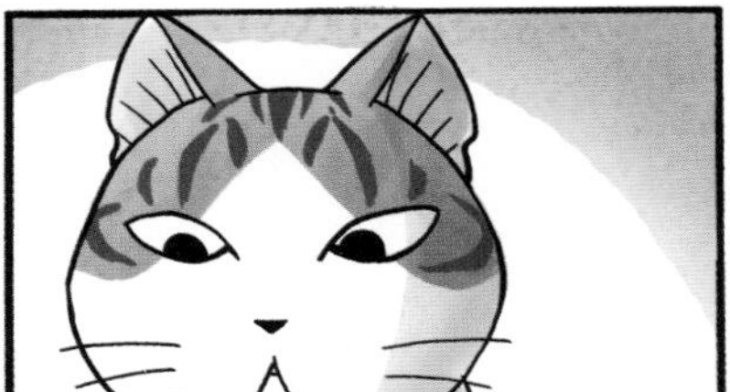
SUCH HIGH SPIRITS.

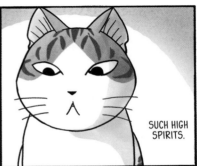

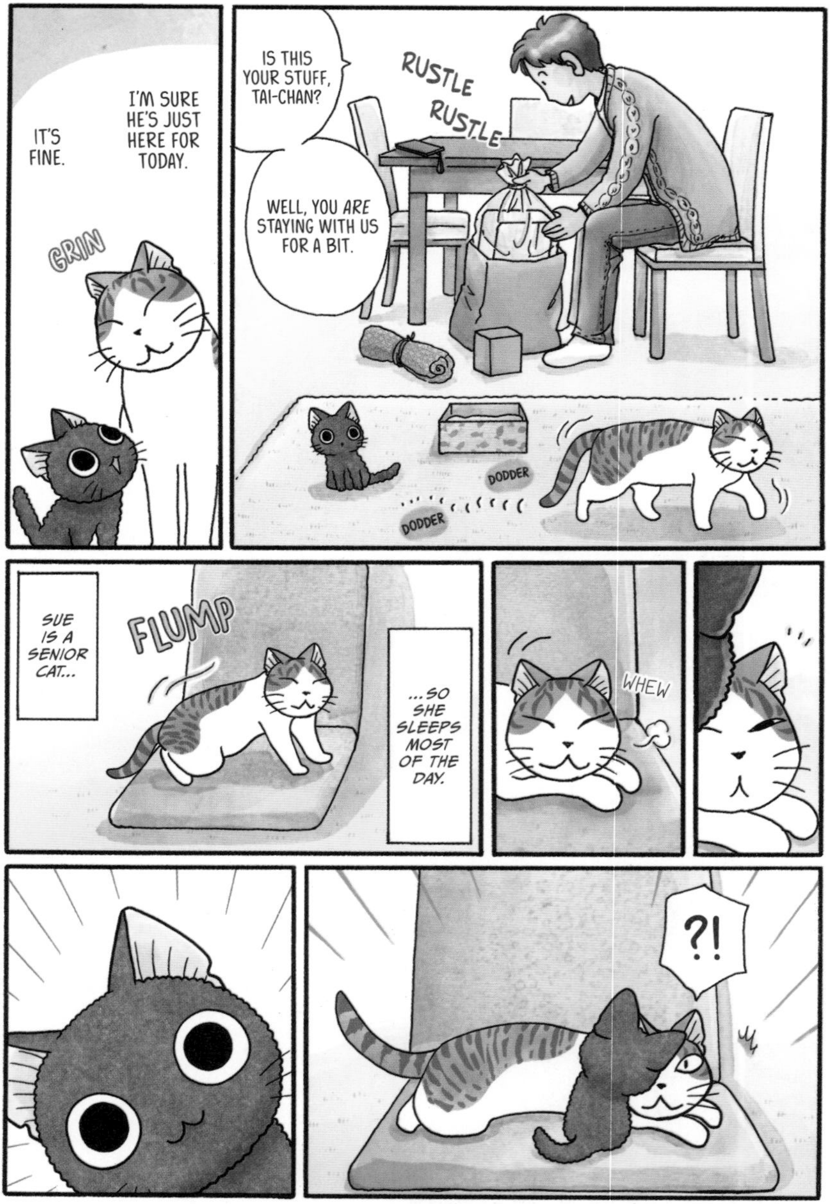
I'M SURE HE'S JUST HERE FOR TODAY.
IT'S FINE.
GRIN
IS THIS YOUR STUFF, TAI-CHAN?
WELL, YOU ARE STAYING WITH US FOR A BIT.
RUSTLE
RUSTLE
DODDER
DODDER
SUE IS A SENIOR CAT...
FLUMP
...SO SHE SLEEPS MOST OF THE DAY.
WHEW
?!

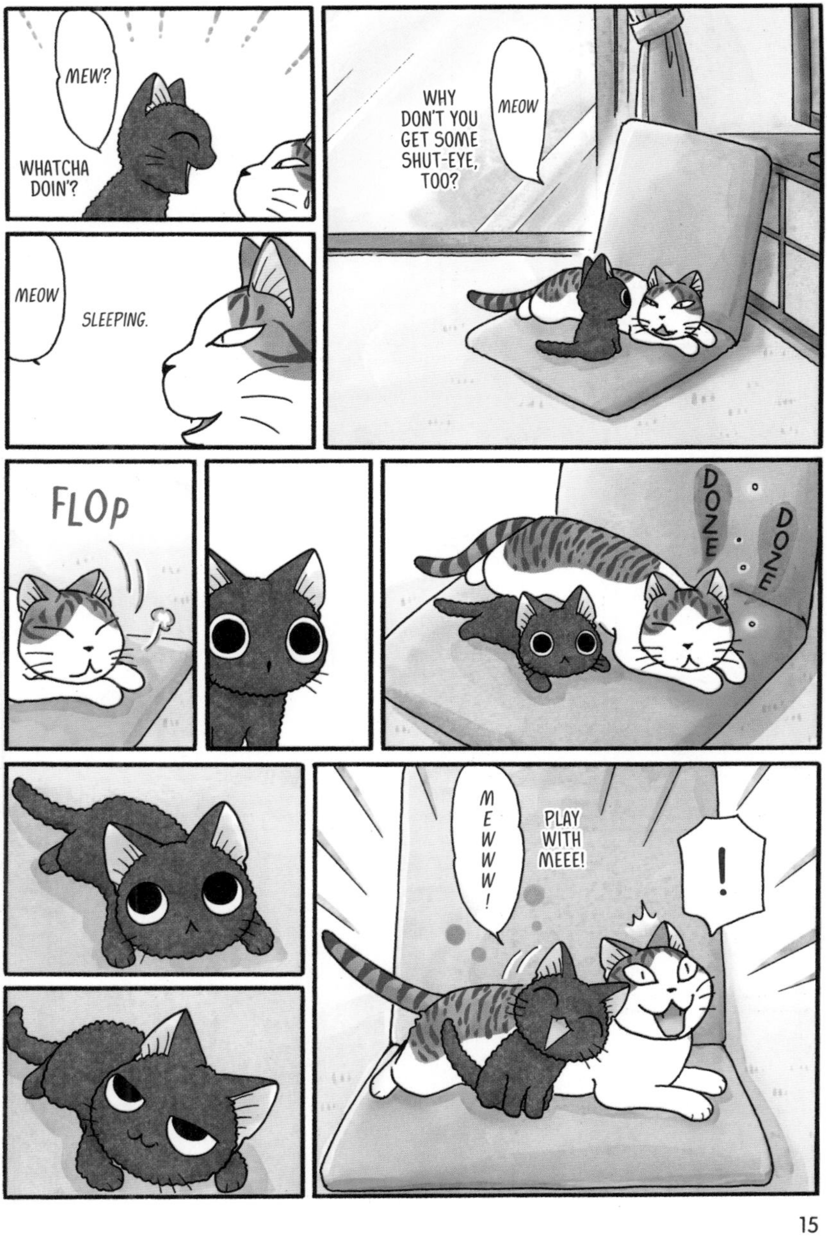

MEW?
WHATCHA DOIN'?
MEOW
SLEEPING.
WHY DON'T YOU GET SOME SHUT-EYE, TOO?
MEOW
FLOP
DOZE
DOZE
MEWWW!
PLAY WITH MEEE!
!

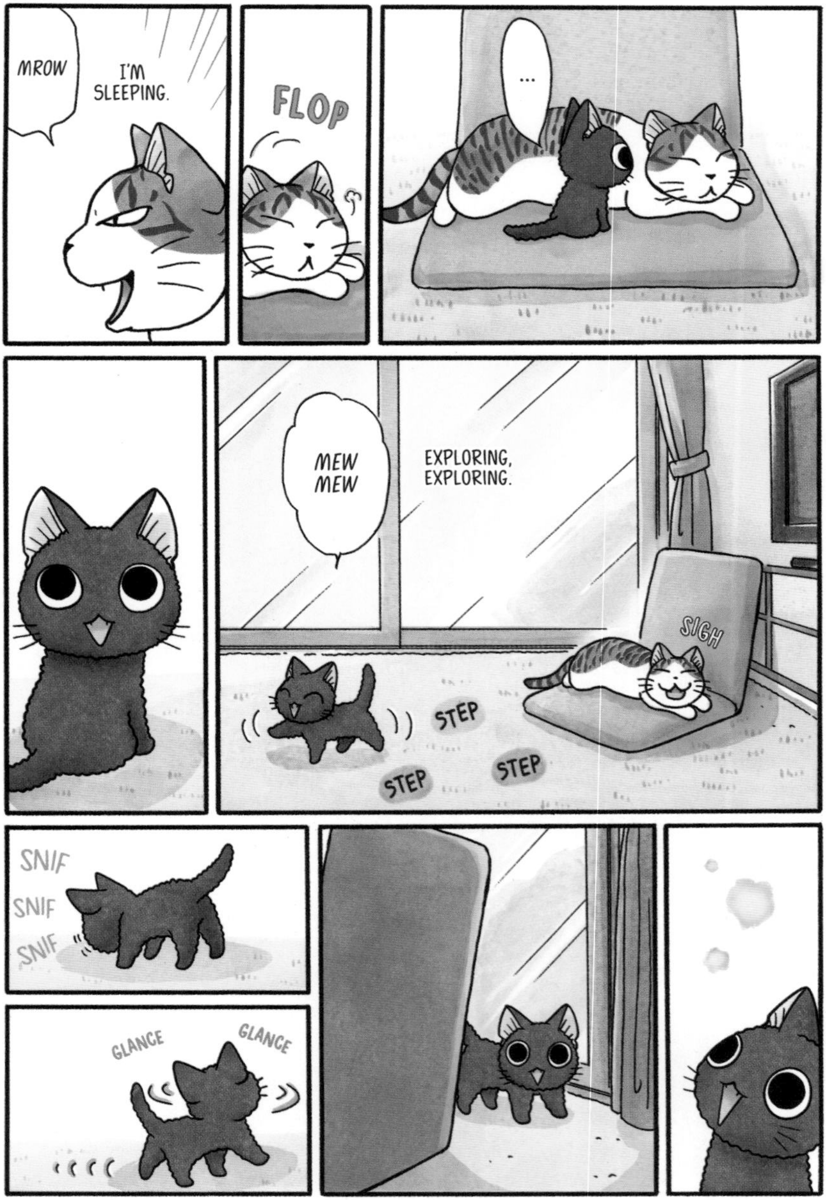
MROW
I'M SLEEPING.
FLOP
...
MEW MEW
EXPLORING, EXPLORING.
SIGH
STEP
STEP
STEP
SNIF
SNIF
SNIF
GLANCE
GLANCE

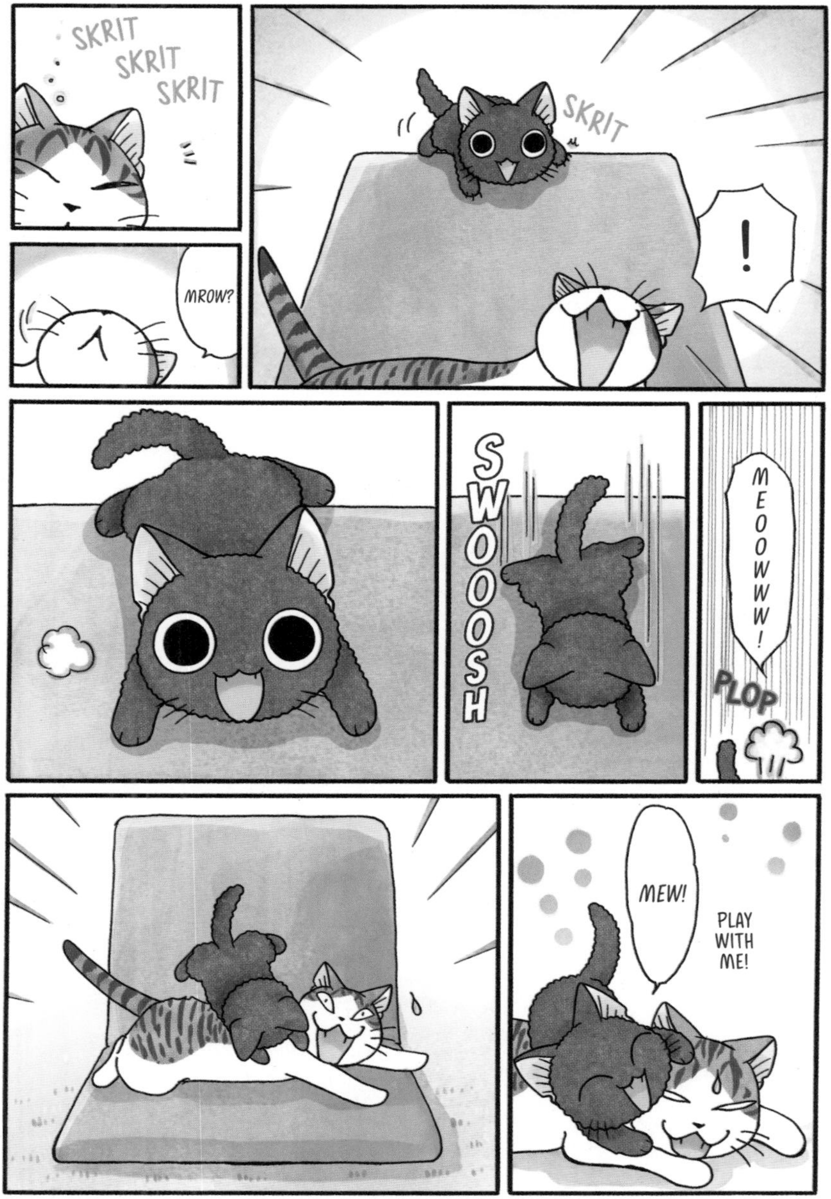
SKRIT
SKRIT
SKRIT
MROW?
SKRIT
!
SWOOOOSH
MEOOWWW!
PLOP
MEW!
PLAY WITH ME!

SHOVE

TUMBLE

PERK!

WANNA PLAY?!

MEWW!

YOU GUYS OKAY?

DING ♪

OH, IT'S MOM.

NATSUKI, HOW ARE YOU? I'M FINALLY GETTING USED TO OUR NEW PLACE. YOUR FATHER'S DOING WELL, TOO!

HOW'S SUE-CHAN? ♡

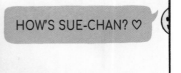
HOW'S SUE-CHAN? ♡

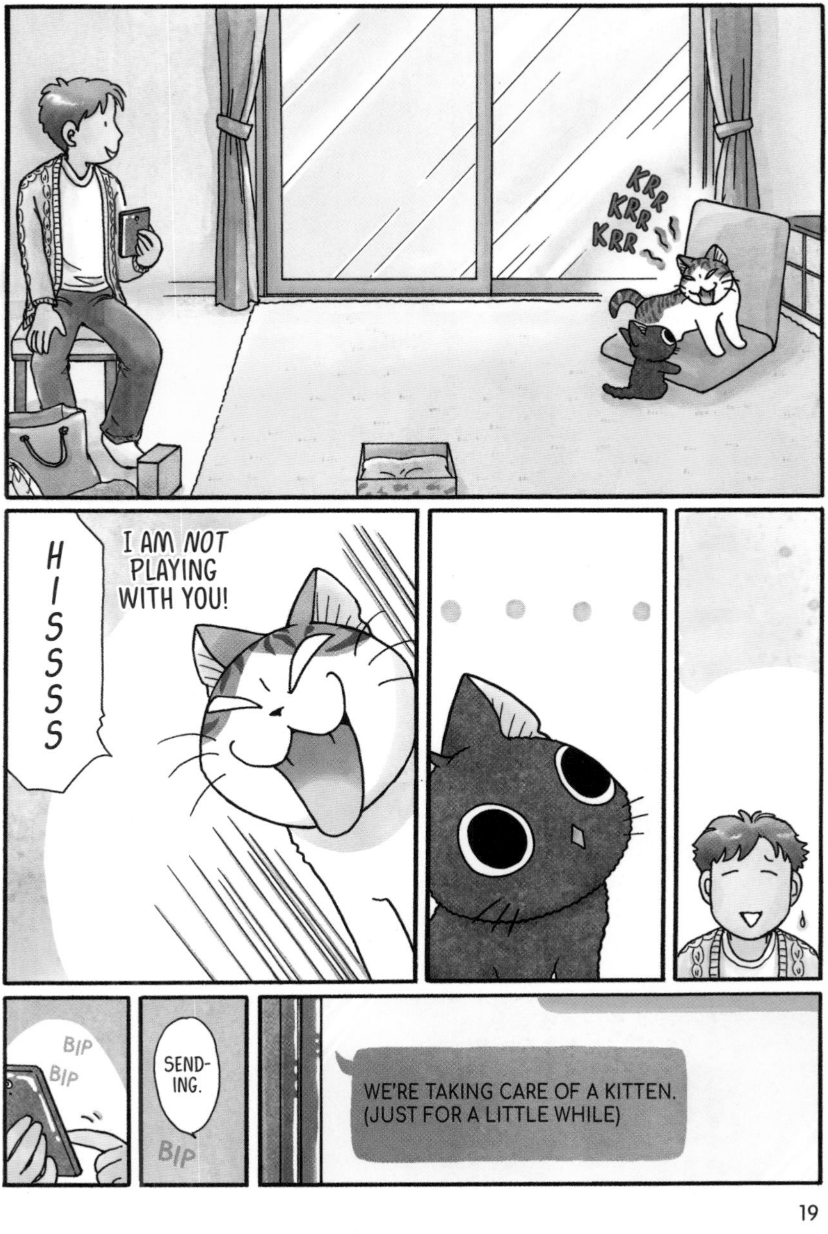
KRR KRR KRR
HISSSS
I AM *NOT* PLAYING WITH YOU!
• • • •
BIP BIP
SEND-ING.
BIP
WE'RE TAKING CARE OF A KITTEN. (JUST FOR A LITTLE WHILE)

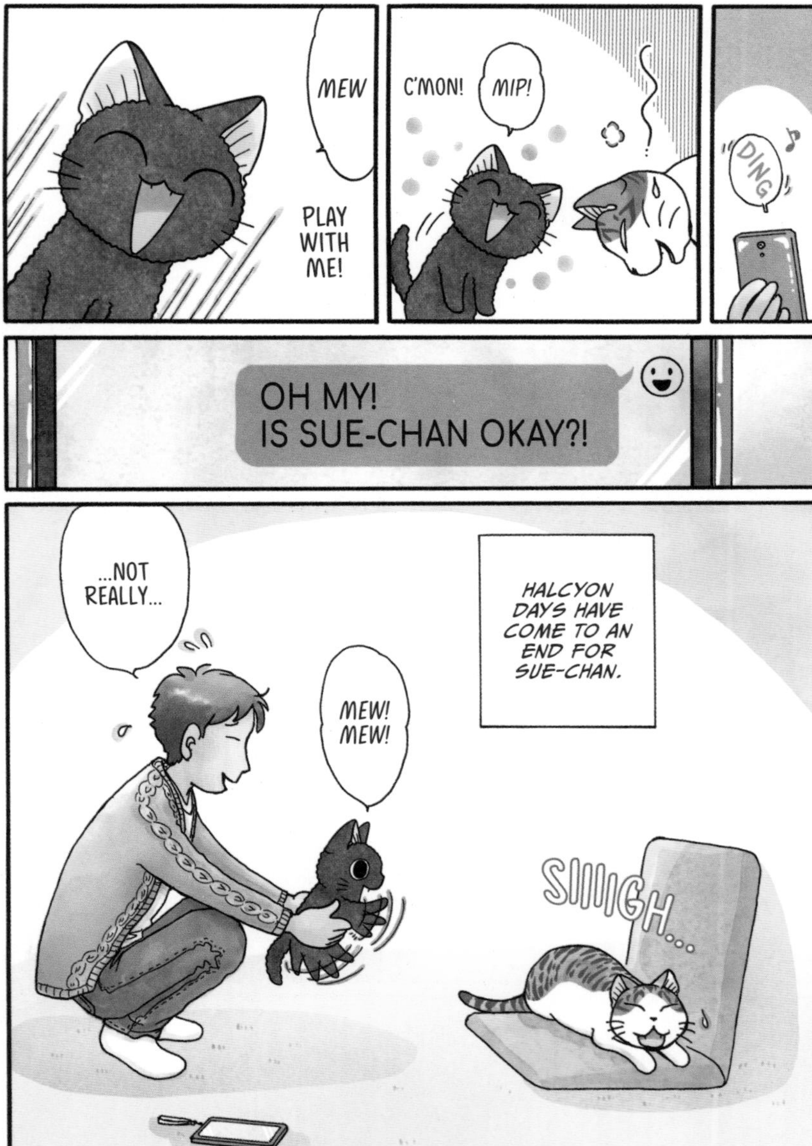
MEW
PLAY WITH ME!
C'MON!
MIP!
DING
OH MY! IS SUE-CHAN OKAY?!
...NOT REALLY...
MEW! MEW!
HALCYON DAYS HAVE COME TO AN END FOR SUE-CHAN.
SIIIGH...

CHAPTER 3 Big Box, Little Box

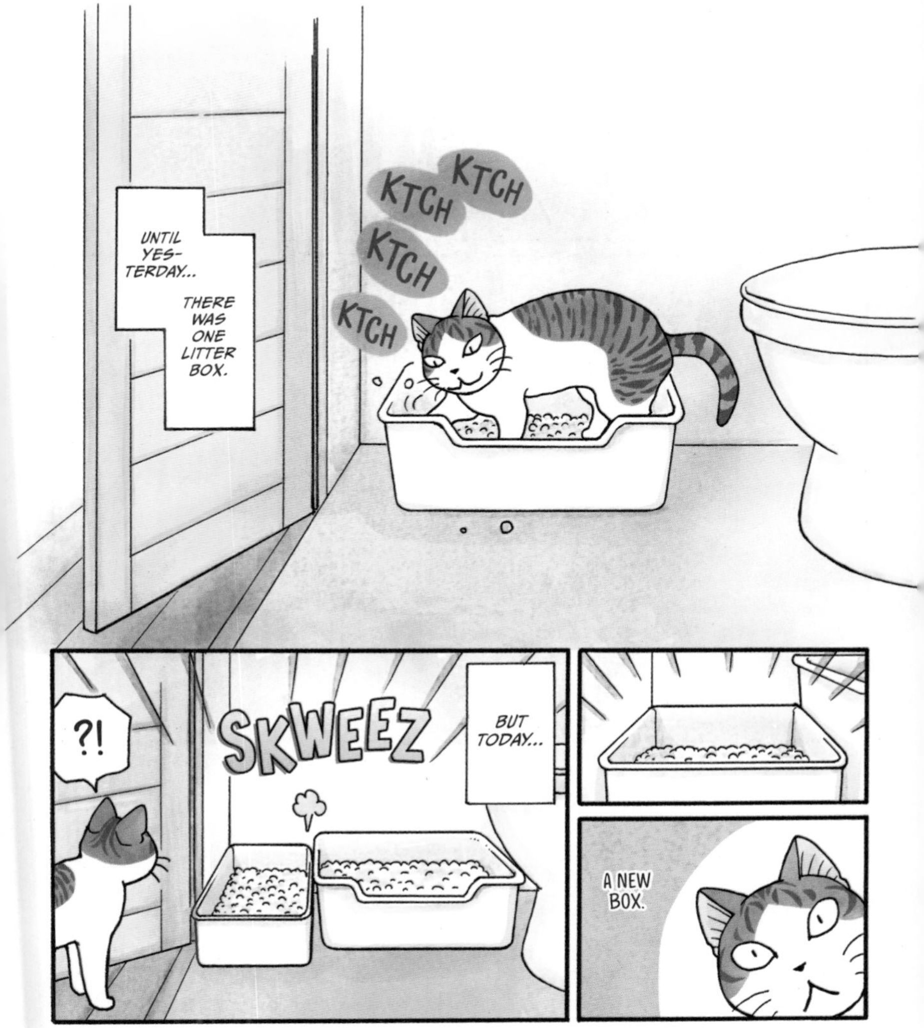
UNTIL YESTERDAY...
THERE WAS ONE LITTER BOX.
KTCH
KTCH
KTCH
KTCH
?!
SKWEEZ
BUT TODAY...
A NEW BOX.

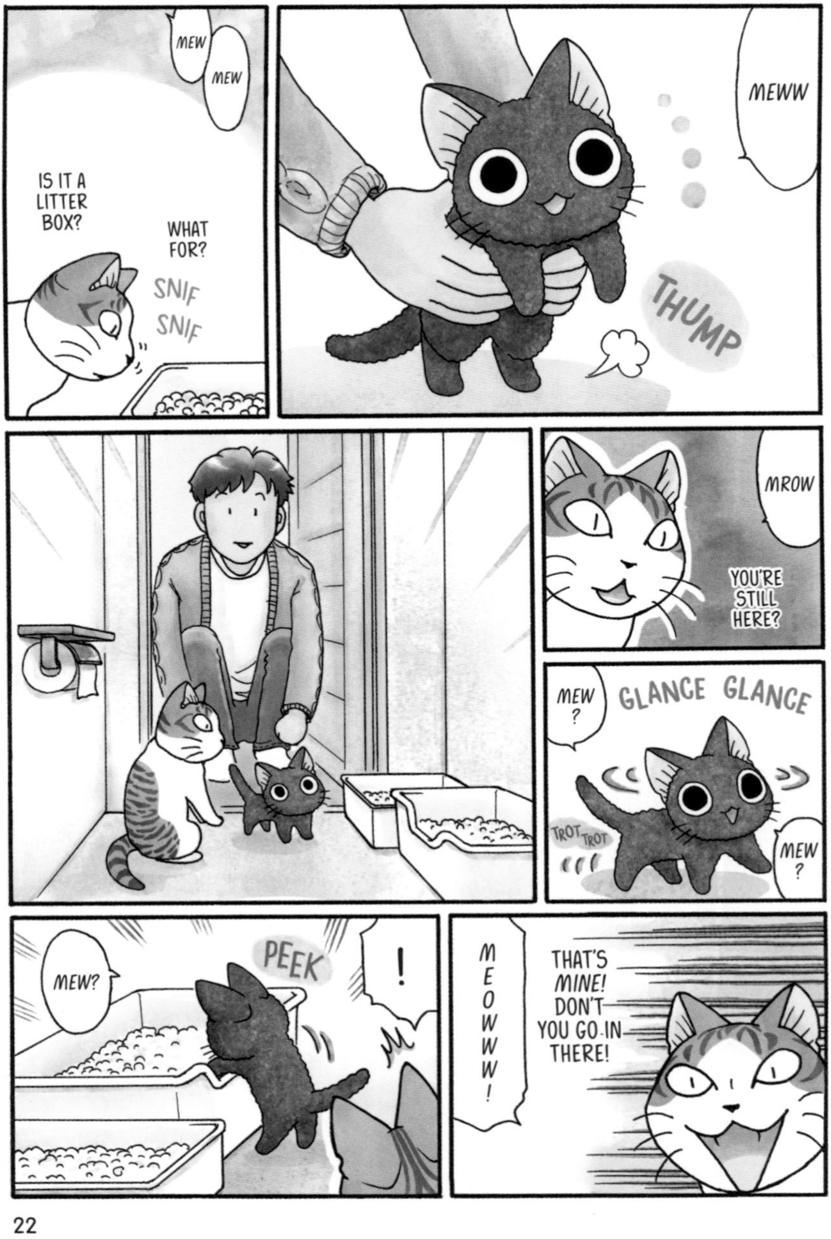
MEW
MEW
IS IT A LITTER BOX?
WHAT FOR?
SNIF
SNIF
MEWW
THUMP
MROW
YOU'RE STILL HERE?
MEW?
GLANCE GLANCE
TROT TROT
MEW?
MEW?
PEEK
!
MEOWWW!
THAT'S MINE! DON'T YOU GO IN THERE!

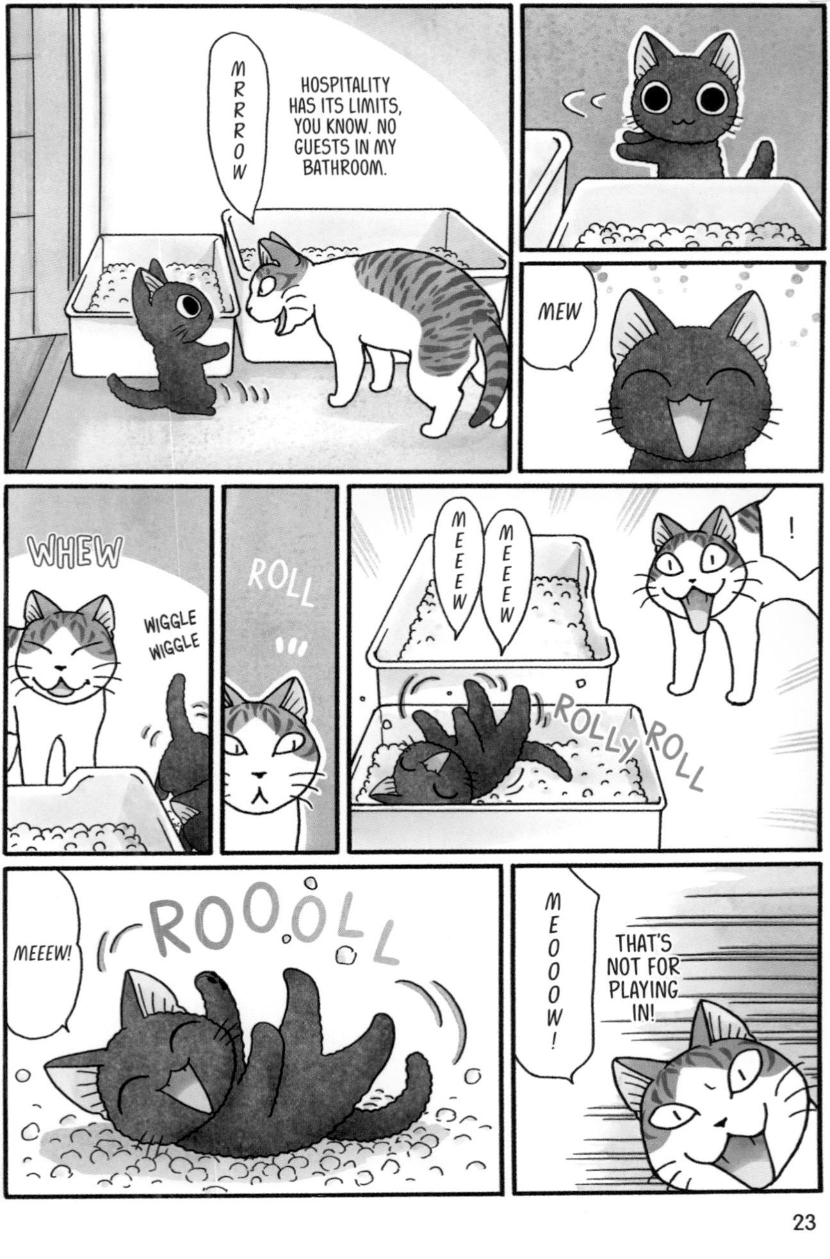
MRRROW
HOSPITALITY HAS ITS LIMITS, YOU KNOW. NO GUESTS IN MY BATHROOM.
MEW
WHEW
WIGGLE WIGGLE
ROLL
MEEEW
MEEEW
!
ROLLY ROLL
MEEEW!
ROOOLL
MEOOOOW!
THAT'S NOT FOR PLAYING IN!

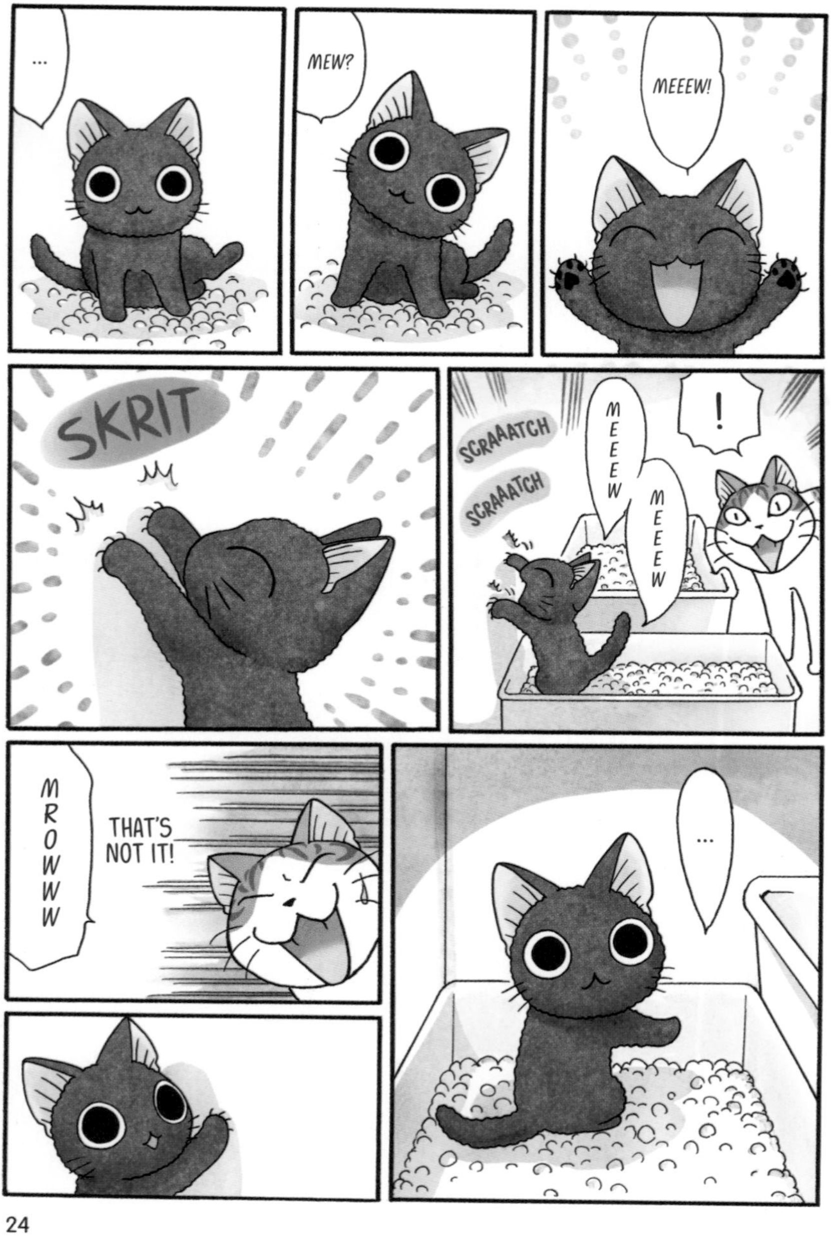
...
MEW?
MEEEW!
SKRIT
SCRAAATCH
SCRAAATCH
MEEEW
MEEEW
!
MROWWW
THAT'S NOT IT!
...

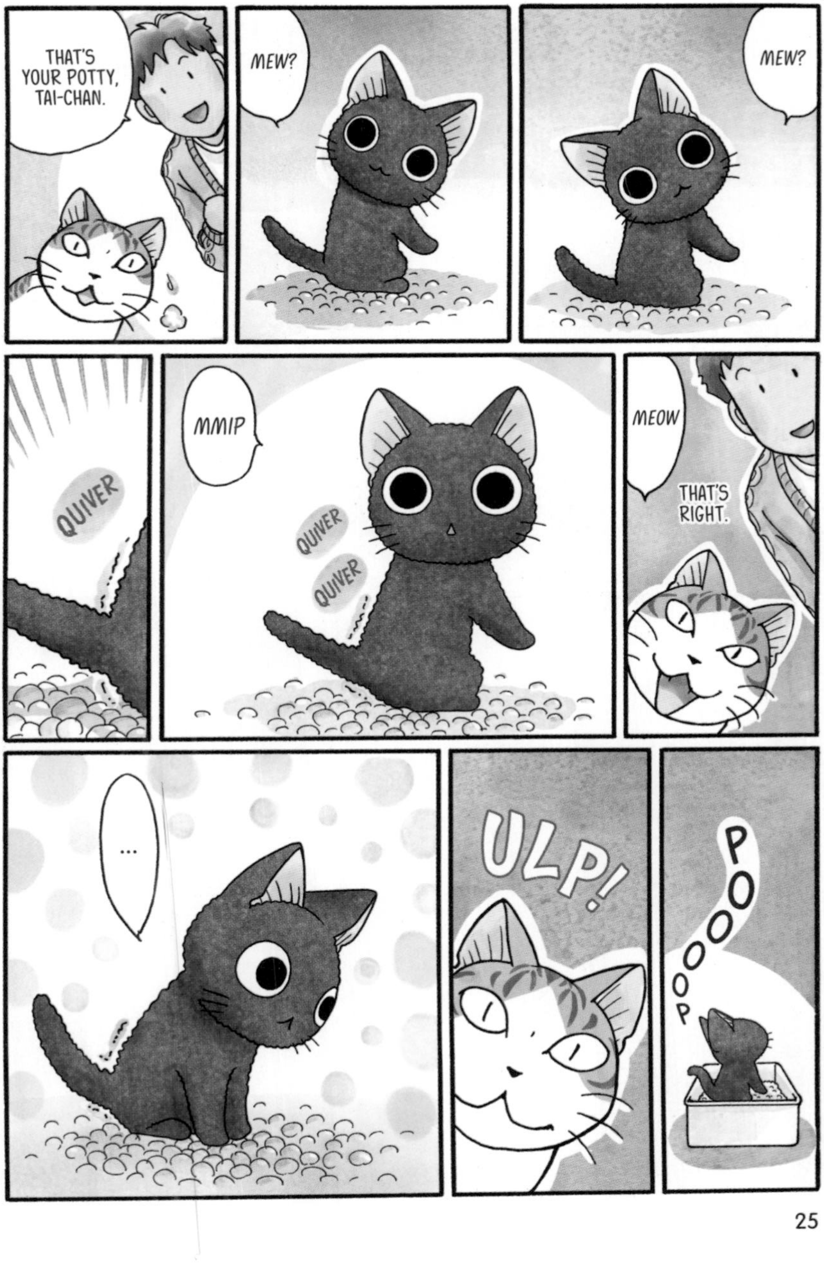

THAT'S YOUR POTTY, TAI-CHAN.
MEW?
MEW?
QUIVER
MMIP
QUIVER
QUIVER
MEOW
THAT'S RIGHT.
...
ULP!
POOOOOP

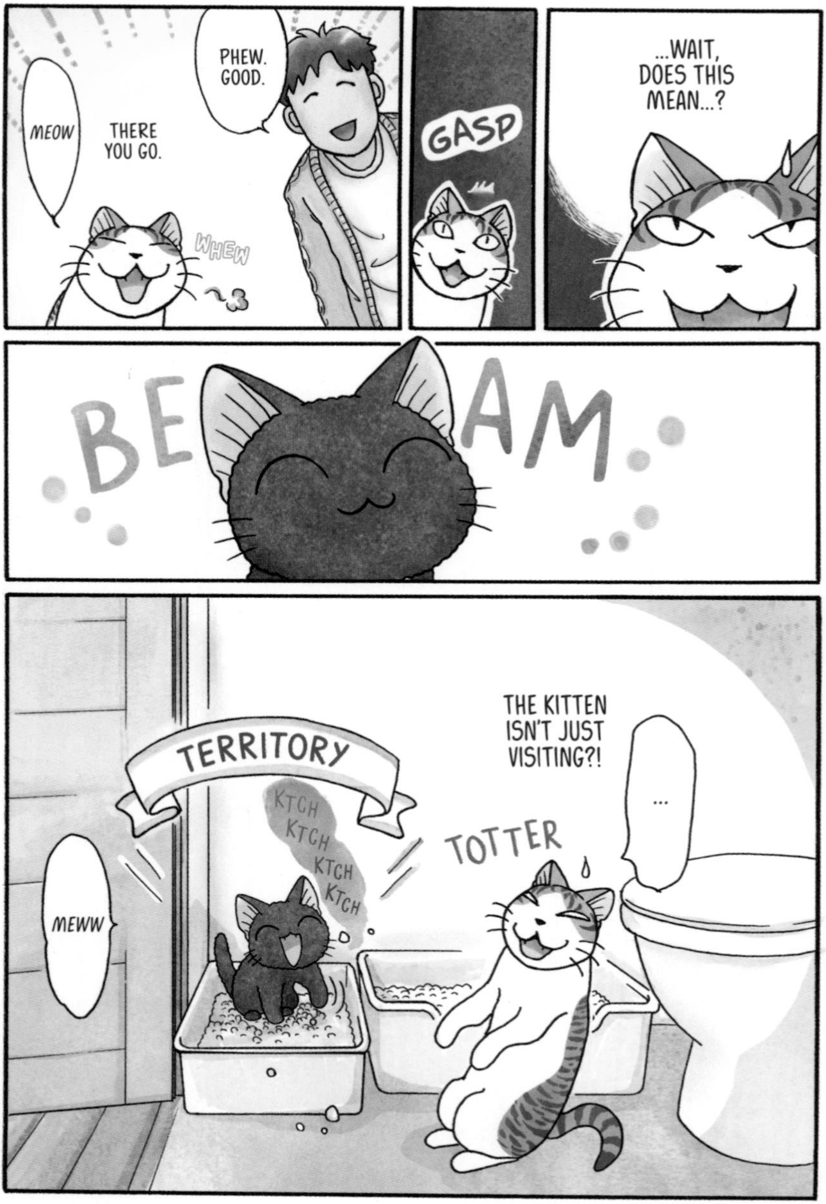
MEOW
THERE YOU GO.
PHEW. GOOD.
WHEW
GASP
...WAIT, DOES THIS MEAN...?
BE AM
TERRITORY
KTCH KTCH KTCH KTCH
MEWW
TOTTER
THE KITTEN ISN'T JUST VISITING?!
...

Sue & Tai-chan

CHAPTER 4 Playful Cat, Sleepy Cat

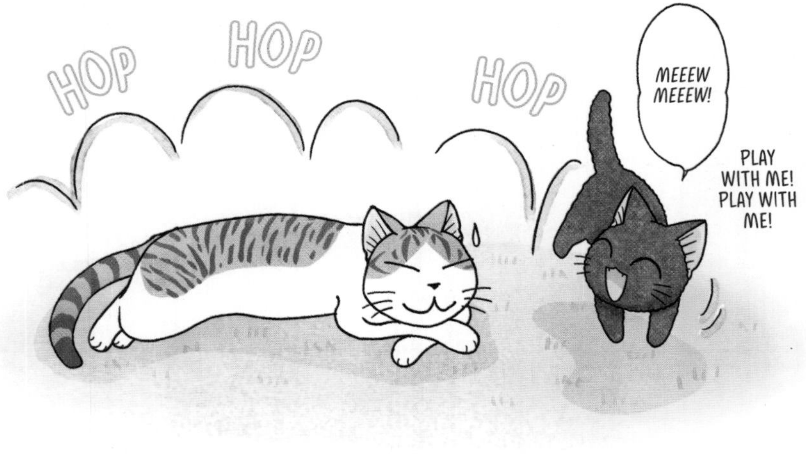
HOP
HOP
HOP
MEEEW MEEEW!
PLAY WITH ME! PLAY WITH ME!

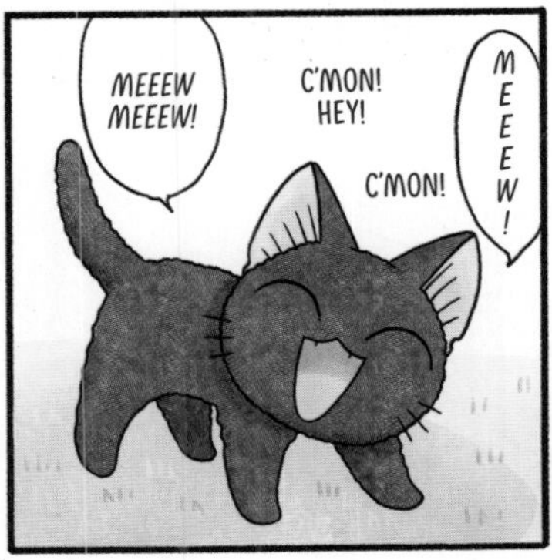
MEEEW MEEEW!
C'MON! HEY!
C'MON!
MEEEW!

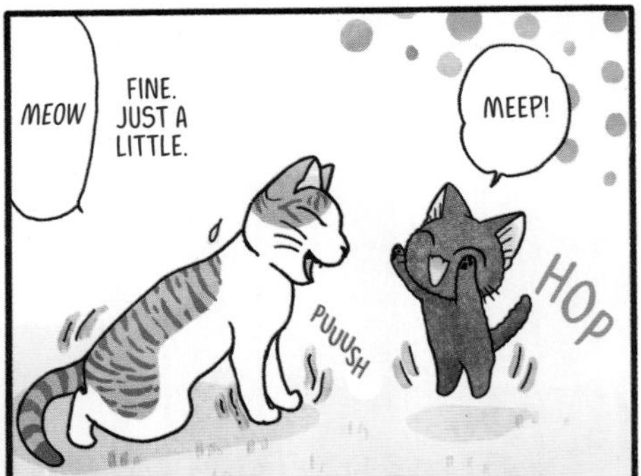
MEOW
FINE. JUST A LITTLE.
PUUUSH
MEEP!
HOP

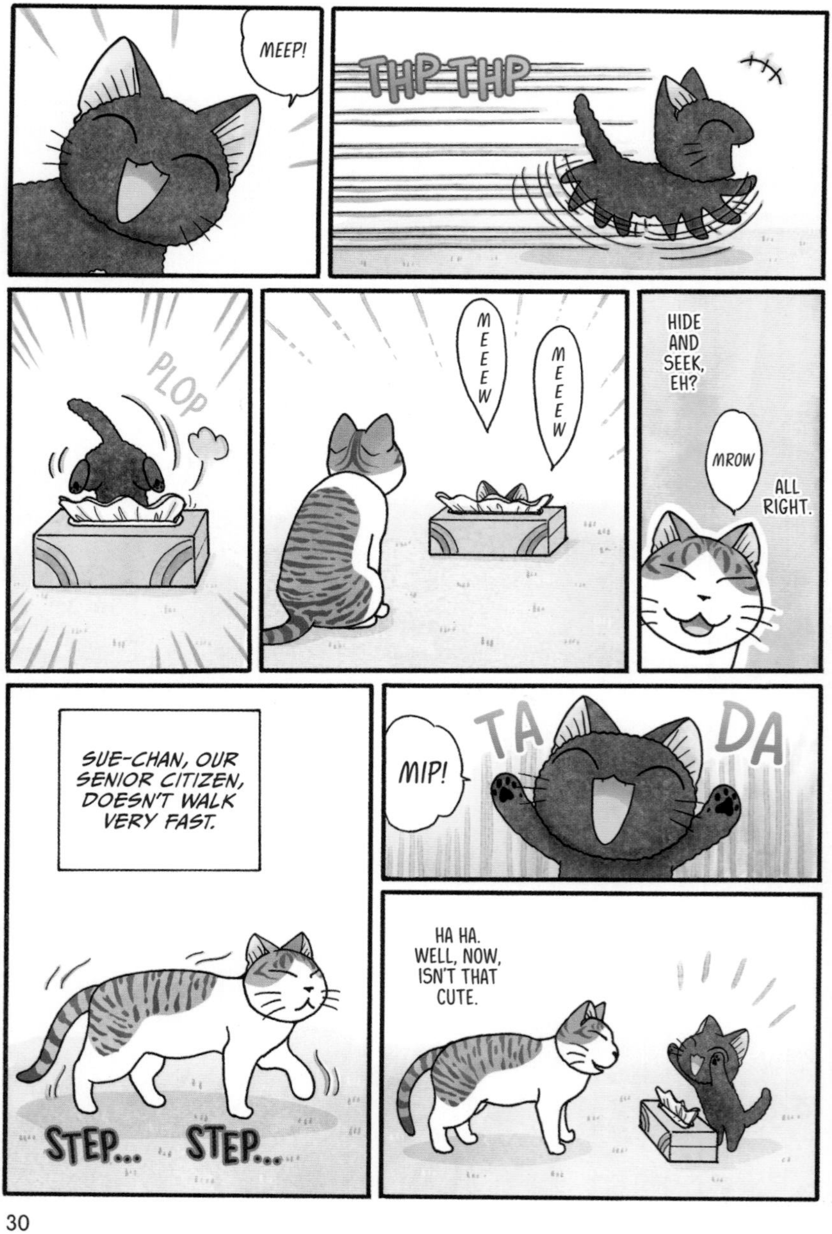
MEEP!
THP THP
PLOP
MEEEW
MEEEW
HIDE AND SEEK, EH?
MROW
ALL RIGHT.
SUE-CHAN, OUR SENIOR CITIZEN, DOESN'T WALK VERY FAST.
STEP... STEP...
TA DA
MIP!
HA HA. WELL, NOW, ISN'T THAT CUTE.

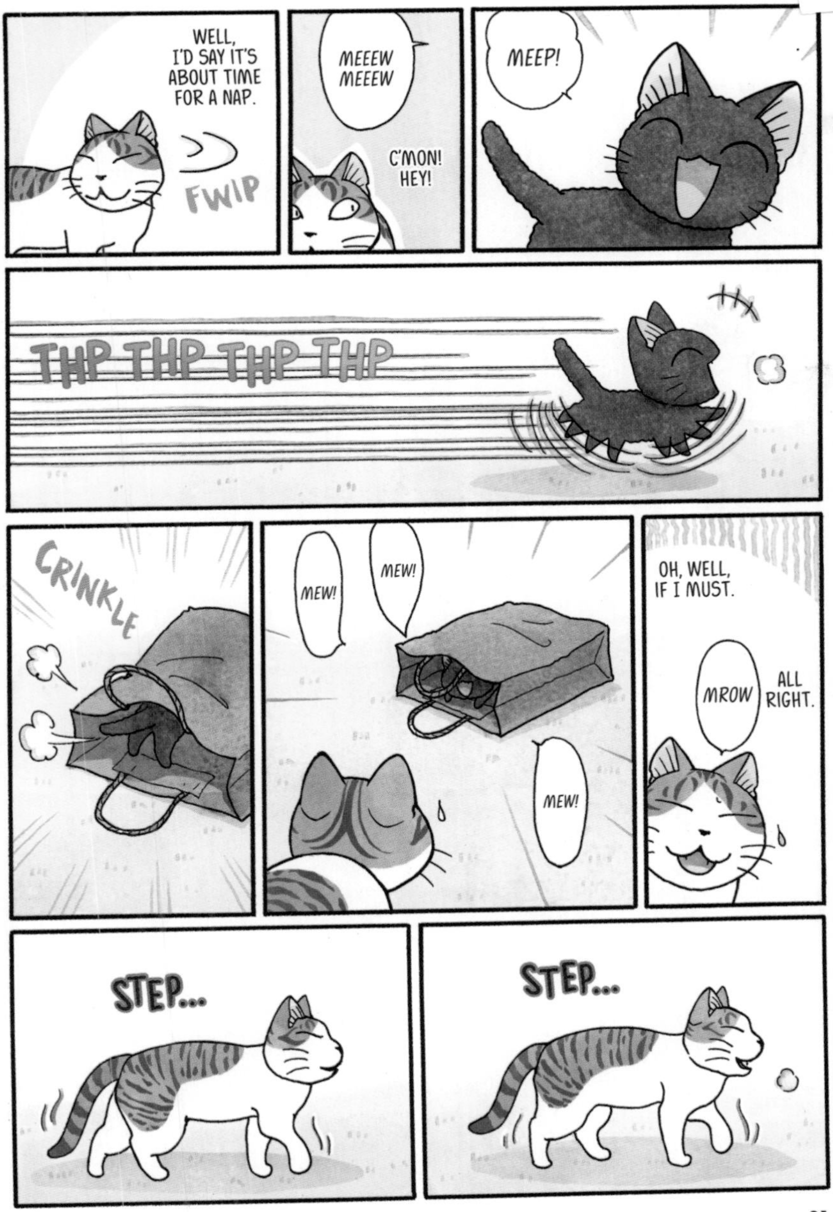
WELL, I'D SAY IT'S ABOUT TIME FOR A NAP.
FWIP
MEEEW MEEEW
C'MON! HEY!
MEEP!
THP THP THP THP
CRINKLE
MEW!
MEW!
MEW!
OH, WELL, IF I MUST.
MROW
ALL RIGHT.
STEP...
STEP...

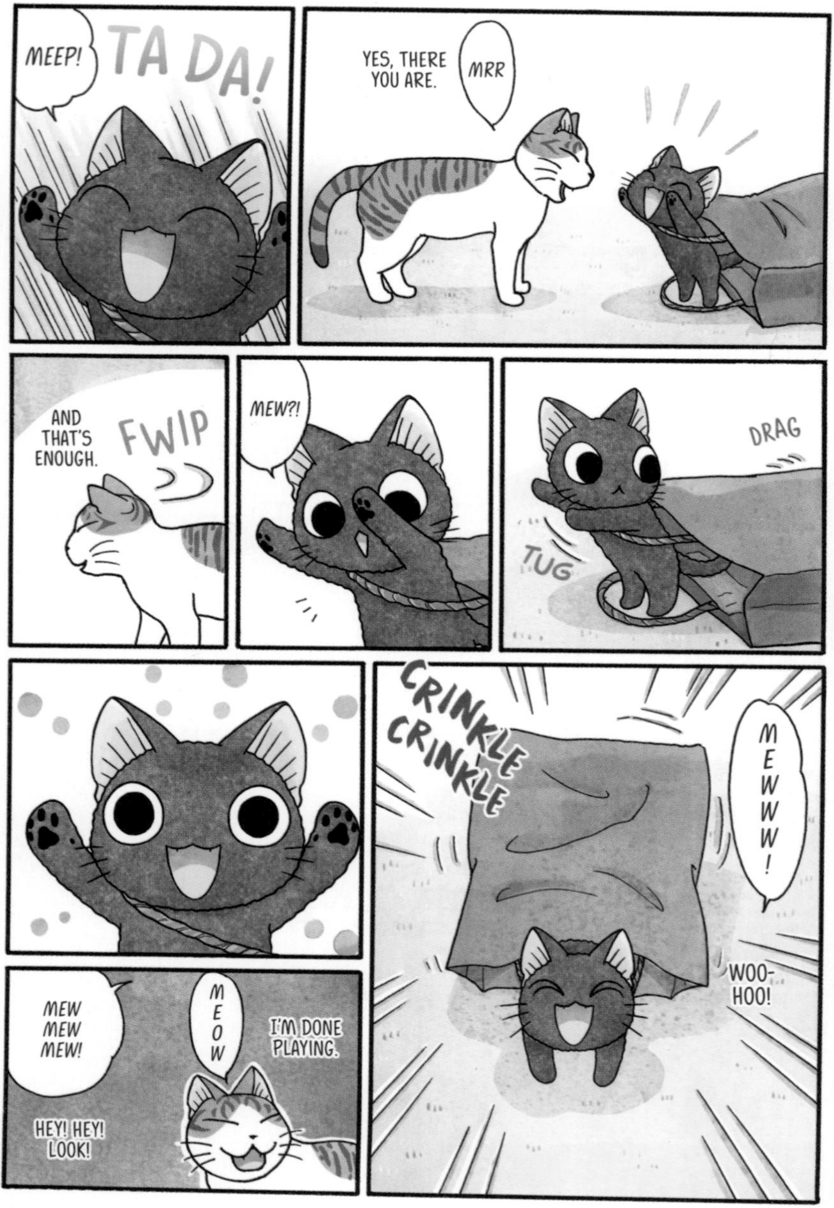
MEEP!
TA DA!
YES, THERE YOU ARE.
MRR
AND THAT'S ENOUGH.
FWIP
MEW?!
DRAG
TUG
MEW MEW MEW!
MEOW
I'M DONE PLAYING.
HEY! HEY! LOOK!
CRINKLE CRINKLE
MEWWWW!
WOO-HOO!

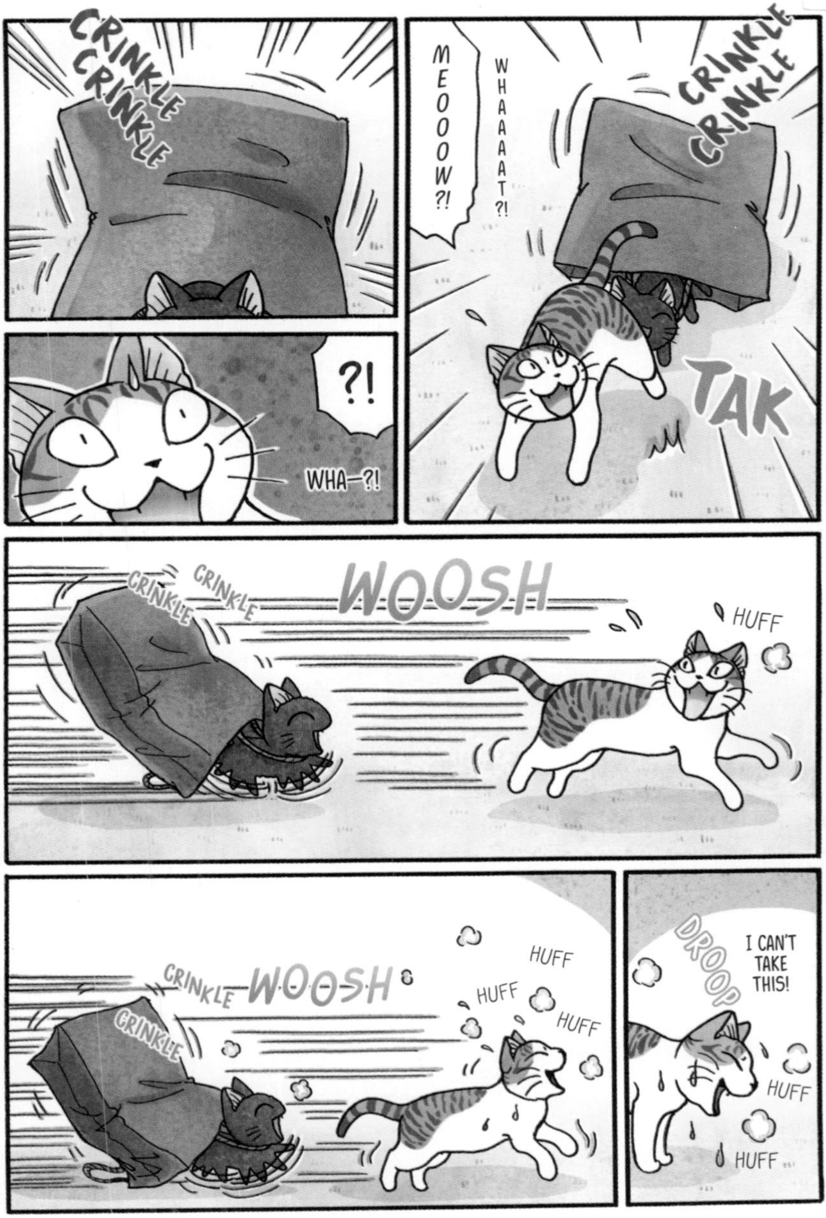
CRINKLE CRINKLE
?!
WHA—?!
MEOOOOW?!
WHAAAAAT?!
CRINKLE CRINKLE
TAK
CRINKLE CRINKLE
WOOSH
HUFF
CRINKLE
WOOSH
CRINKLE
HUFF
HUFF
HUFF
DROOP
I CAN'T TAKE THIS!
HUFF
HUFF

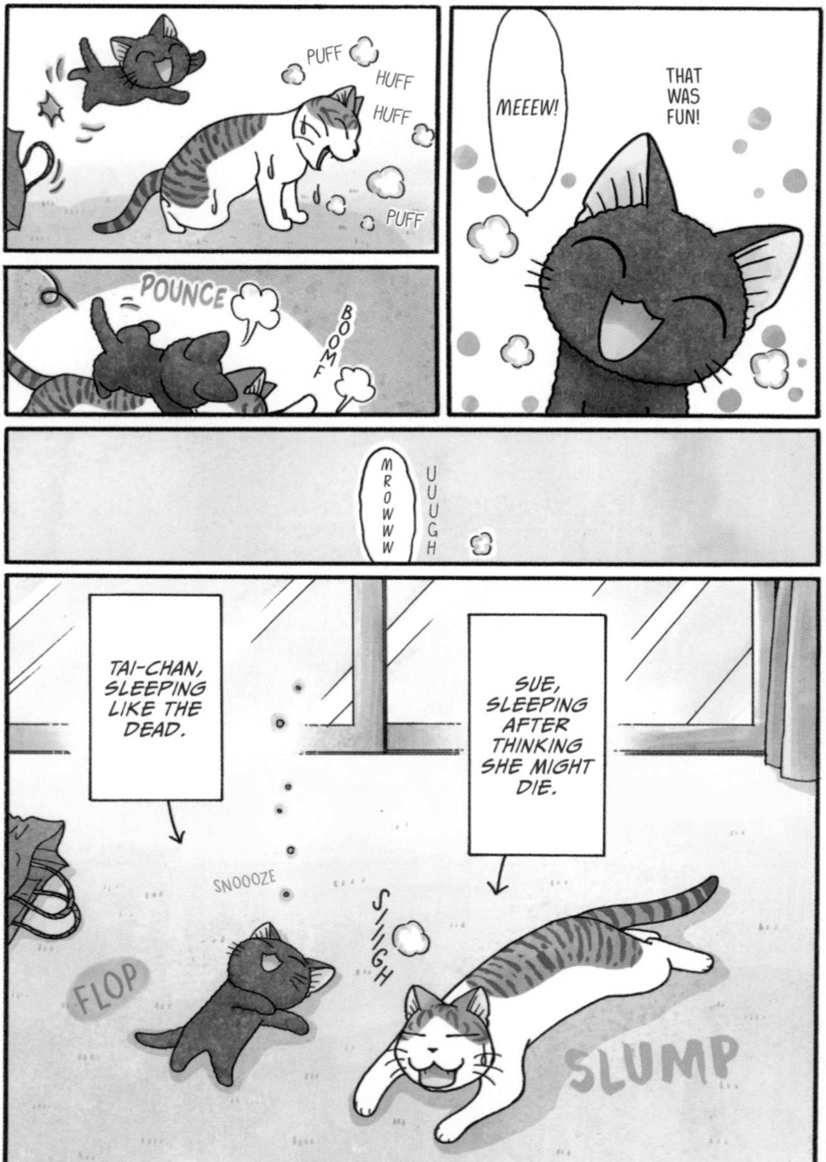
PUFF
HUFF
HUFF
PUFF
POUNCE
BOOMF
MEEEW!
THAT WAS FUN!
MROWWW
UUUGH
TAI-CHAN, SLEEPING LIKE THE DEAD.
SUE, SLEEPING AFTER THINKING SHE MIGHT DIE.
SNOOOZE
SIGH
FLOP
SLUMP

CHAPTER 5 A Kitten Licks to Learn

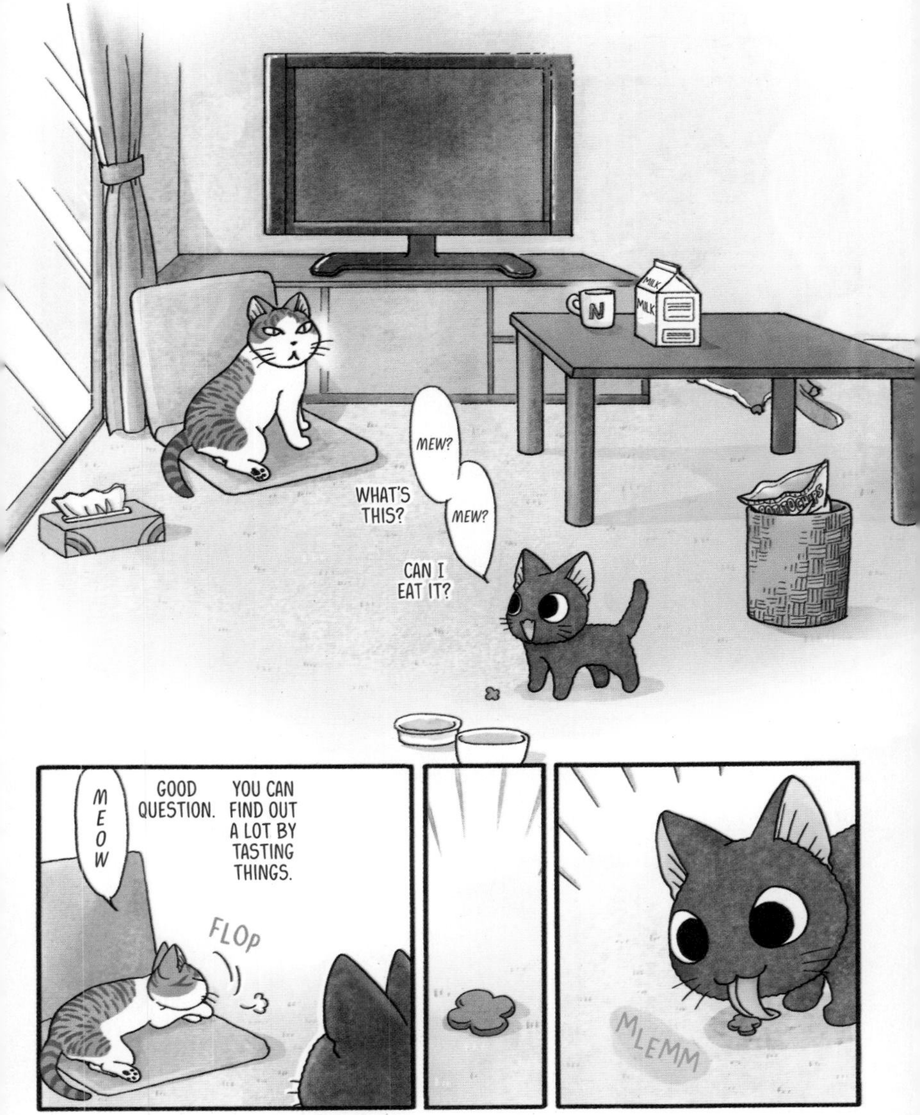
MEW?
WHAT'S THIS?
MEW?
CAN I EAT IT?
MEOW
GOOD QUESTION.
YOU CAN FIND OUT A LOT BY TASTING THINGS.
FLOP
MLEMM

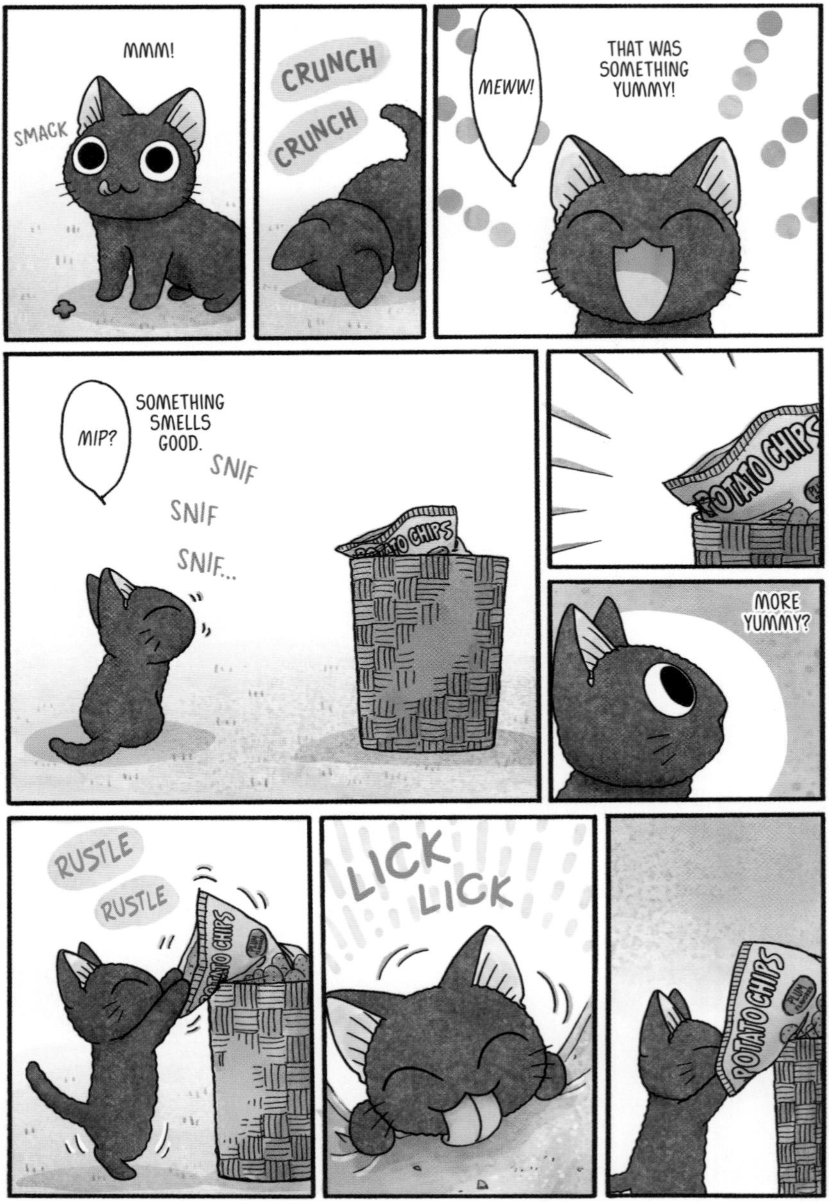
MMM!
SMACK
CRUNCH
CRUNCH
MEWW!
THAT WAS SOMETHING YUMMY!
MIP?
SOMETHING SMELLS GOOD.
SNIF
SNIF
SNIF...
POTATO CHIPS
POTATO CHIPS
MORE YUMMY?
RUSTLE
RUSTLE
POTATO CHIPS
LICK
LICK
POTATO CHIPS
PLUM

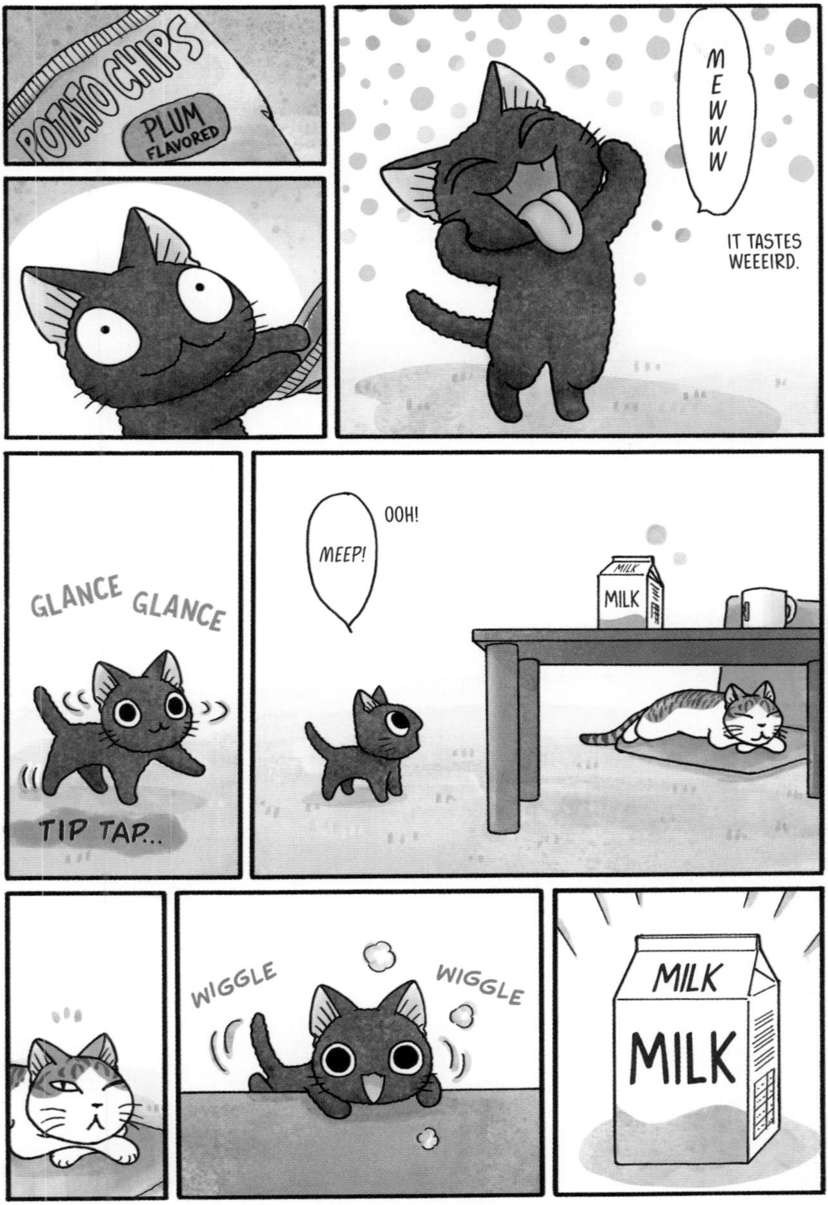
POTATO CHIPS
PLUM FLAVORED
MEWWW
IT TASTES WEEEIRD.
GLANCE GLANCE
TIP TAP...
MEEP!
OOH!
MILK
MILK
WIGGLE WIGGLE
MILK
MILK

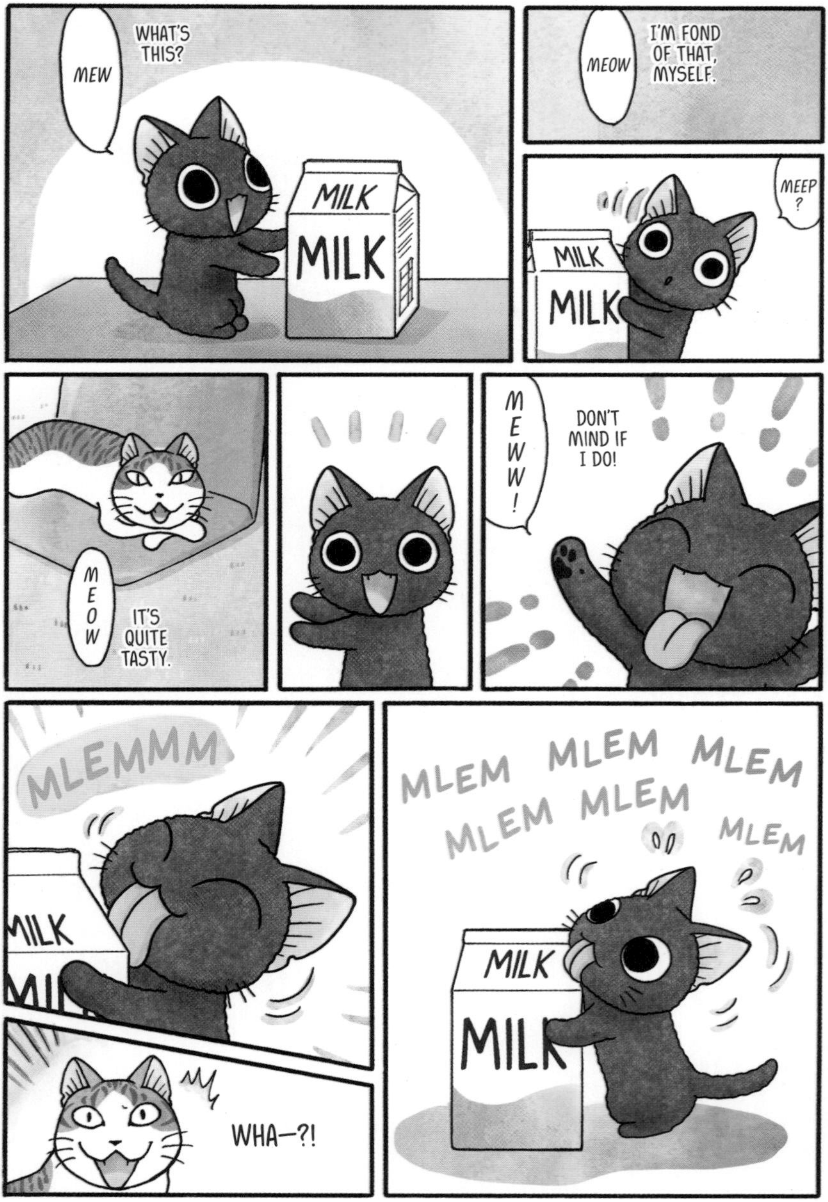

MEW
WHAT'S THIS?
MEOW
I'M FOND OF THAT, MYSELF.
MEEP?
MILK
MILK
MEOW
IT'S QUITE TASTY.
MEWW!
DON'T MIND IF I DO!
MLEMMM
WHA—?!
MLEM MLEM MLEM
MLEM MLEM
MLEM
MILK
MILK

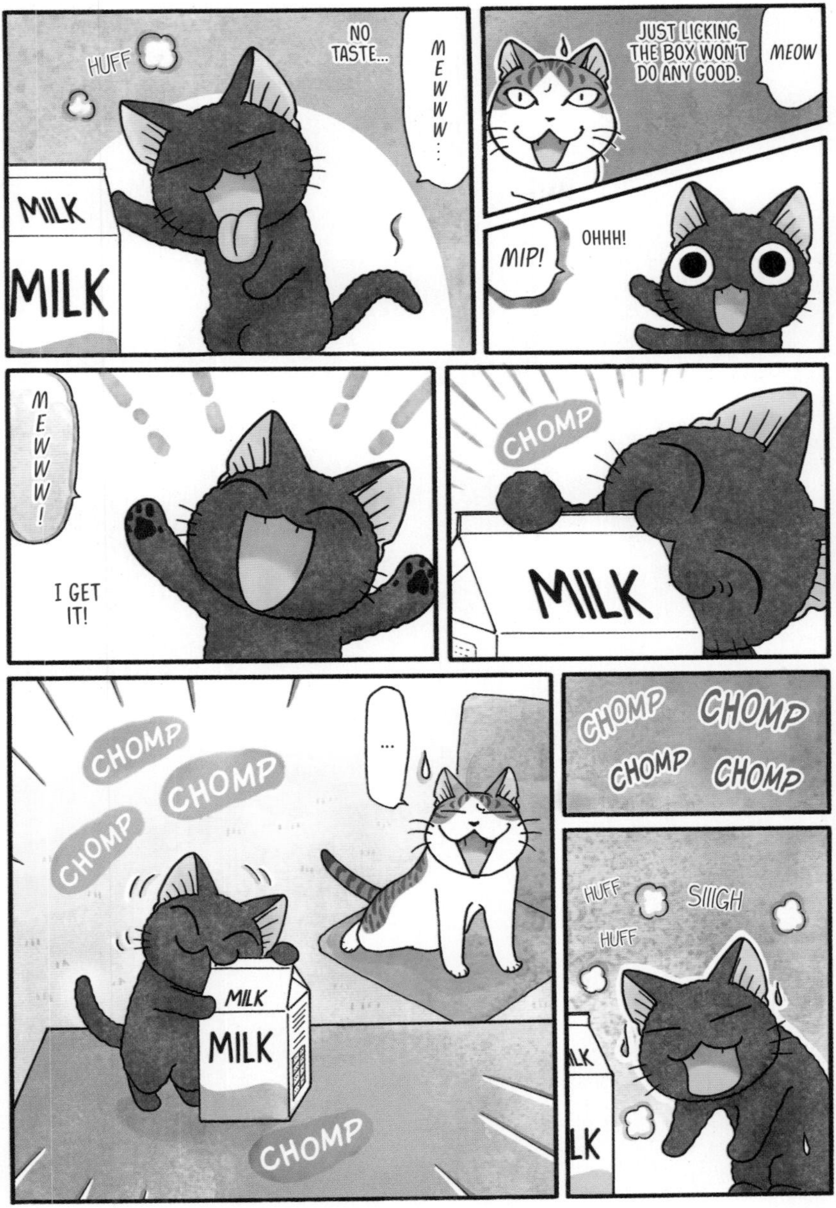
HUFF
NO TASTE...
MEWWW...
MILK
MILK
JUST LICKING THE BOX WON'T DO ANY GOOD.
MEOW
MIP!
OHHH!
MEWWW!
I GET IT!
CHOMP
MILK
CHOMP
CHOMP
CHOMP
...
MILK
MILK
CHOMP
CHOMP
CHOMP
CHOMP
CHOMP
HUFF
SIIIGH
HUFF
LK
LK

MEW

THAT'S NOT TASTY.

TMP

TEK TEK TEK

MIP?

OOH!

WHAT ABOUT THIS ONE?

MEWW?

LICK LICK

...?

MROWW?

GOODNESS, WHAT ARE YOU DOING?

MEOW

YOU CAN'T EAT THAT THING.

40

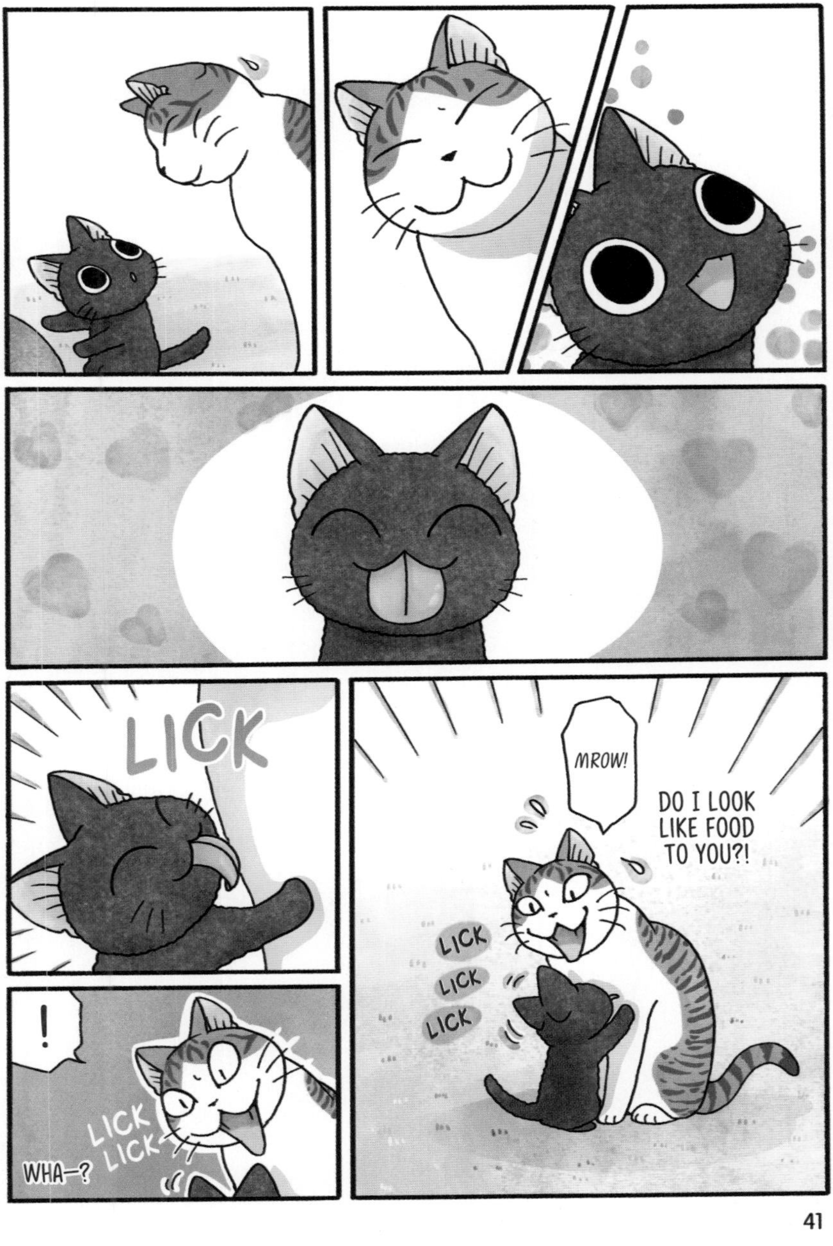
LICK
!
LICK
LICK
WHA–?
MROW!
DO I LOOK LIKE FOOD TO YOU?!
LICK
LICK
LICK

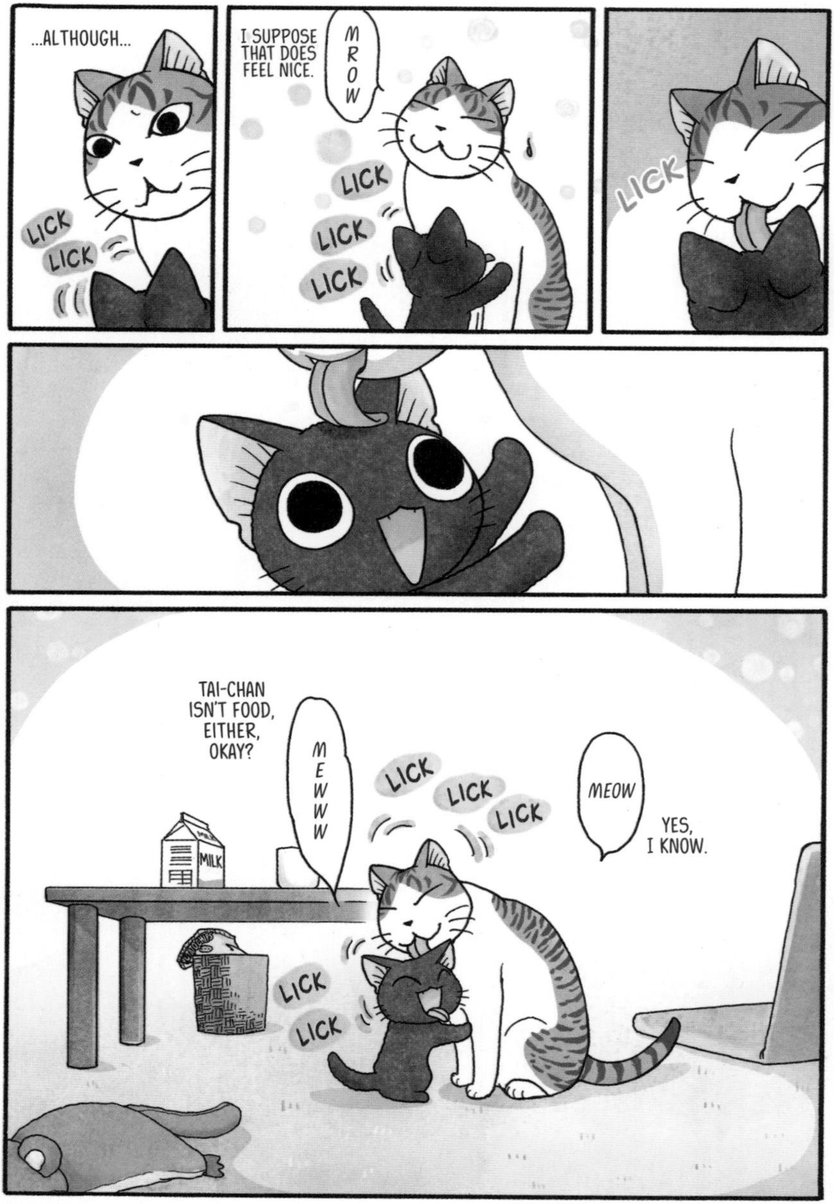
...ALTHOUGH...
LICK
LICK
I SUPPOSE THAT DOES FEEL NICE.
MROW
LICK
LICK
LICK
LICK
TAI-CHAN ISN'T FOOD, EITHER, OKAY?
MEWWW
LICK
LICK
LICK
MEOW
YES, I KNOW.
MILK
LICK
LICK

CHAPTER 6

Feline Face-Washing: Basic Methods

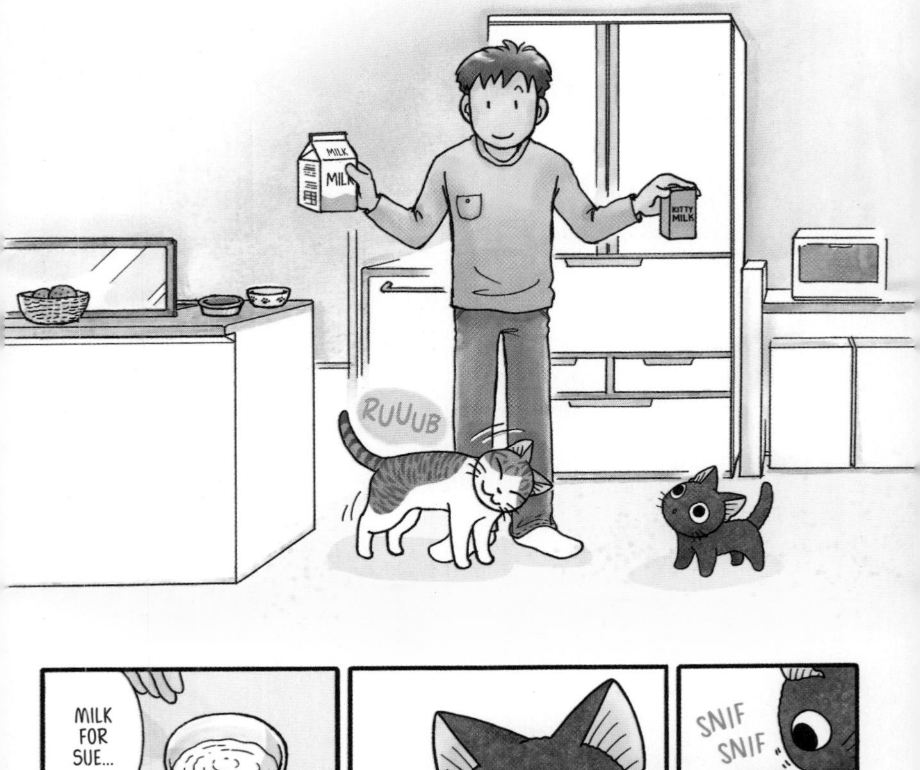
MILK
MILK
KITTY MILK
RUUUB

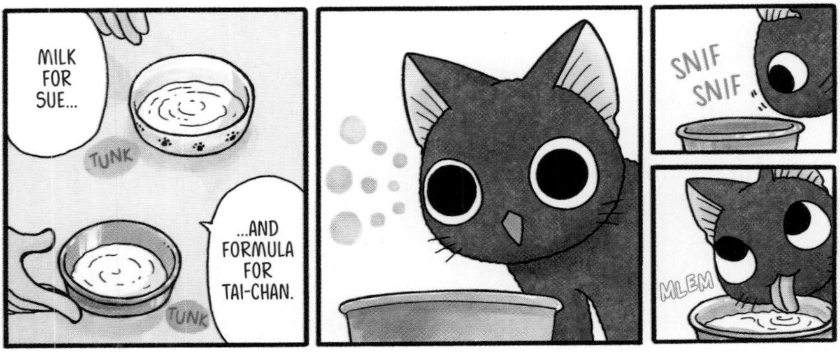
MILK FOR SUE...
TUNK
...AND FORMULA FOR TAI-CHAN.
TUNK
SNIF SNIF
MLEM

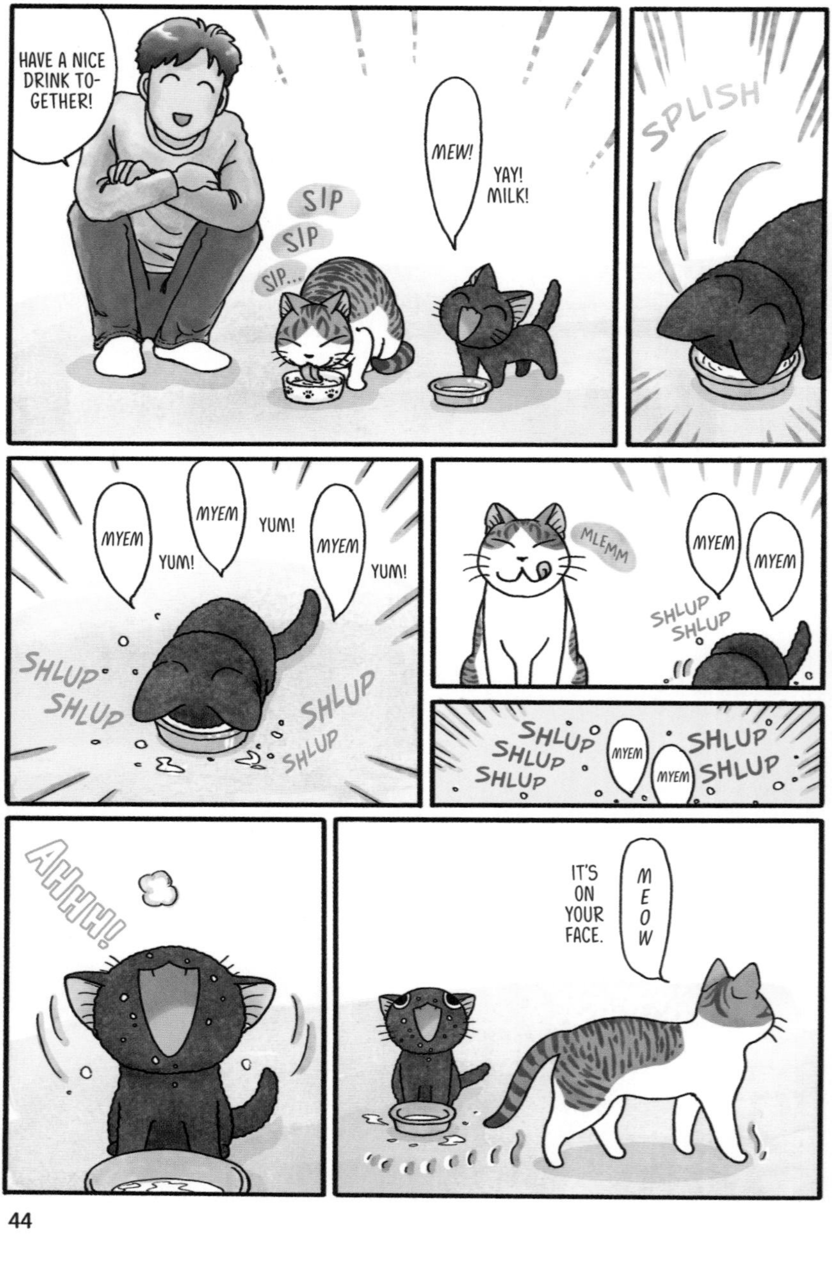
HAVE A NICE DRINK TO-GETHER!
SIP
SIP
SIP...
MEW!
YAY! MILK!
SPLISH
MYEM
YUM!
MYEM
YUM!
MYEM
YUM!
SHLUP
SHLUP
SHLUP
SHLUP
MLEMM
MYEM
MYEM
SHLUP
SHLUP
SHLUP
SHLUP
SHLUP
MYEM
MYEM
SHLUP
SHLUP
AHHH!
IT'S ON YOUR FACE.
MEOW

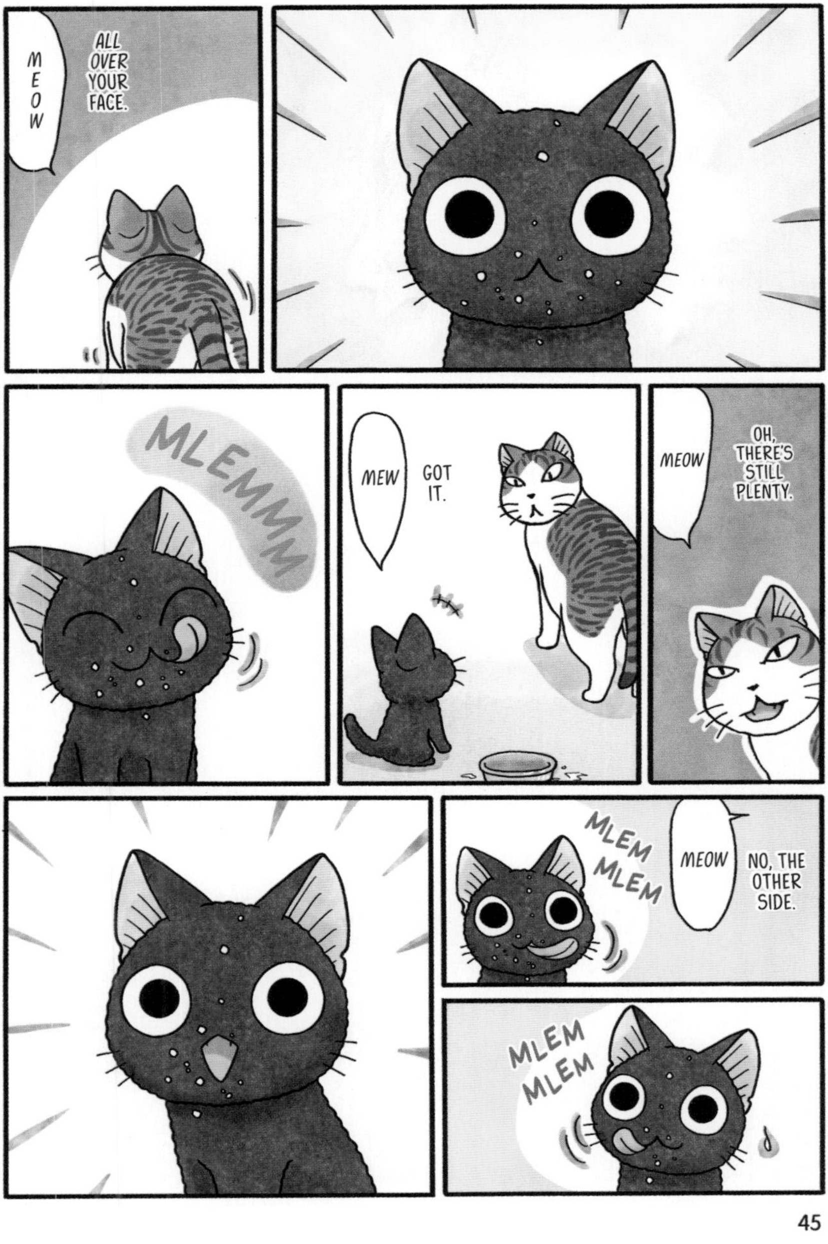
MEOW
ALL OVER YOUR FACE.
MLEMMM
MEW
GOT IT.
MEOW
OH, THERE'S STILL PLENTY.
MLEM MLEM
MEOW
NO, THE OTHER SIDE.
MLEM MLEM

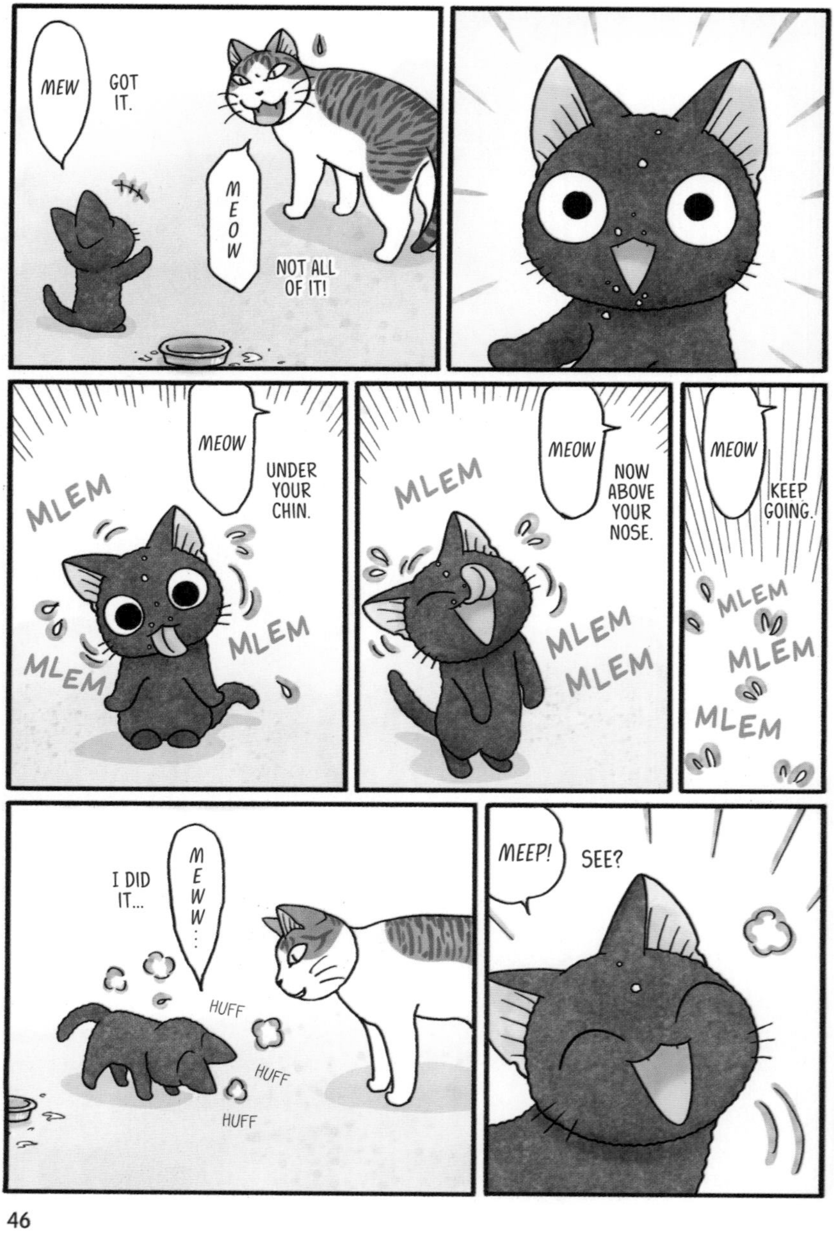
MEW
GOT IT.
MEOW
NOT ALL OF IT!
MEOW
UNDER YOUR CHIN.
MLEM
MLEM
MLEM
MEOW
NOW ABOVE YOUR NOSE.
MLEM
MLEM
MLEM
MEOW
KEEP GOING.
MLEM
MLEM
MLEM
I DID IT...
MEWW...
HUFF
HUFF
HUFF
MEEP!
SEE?

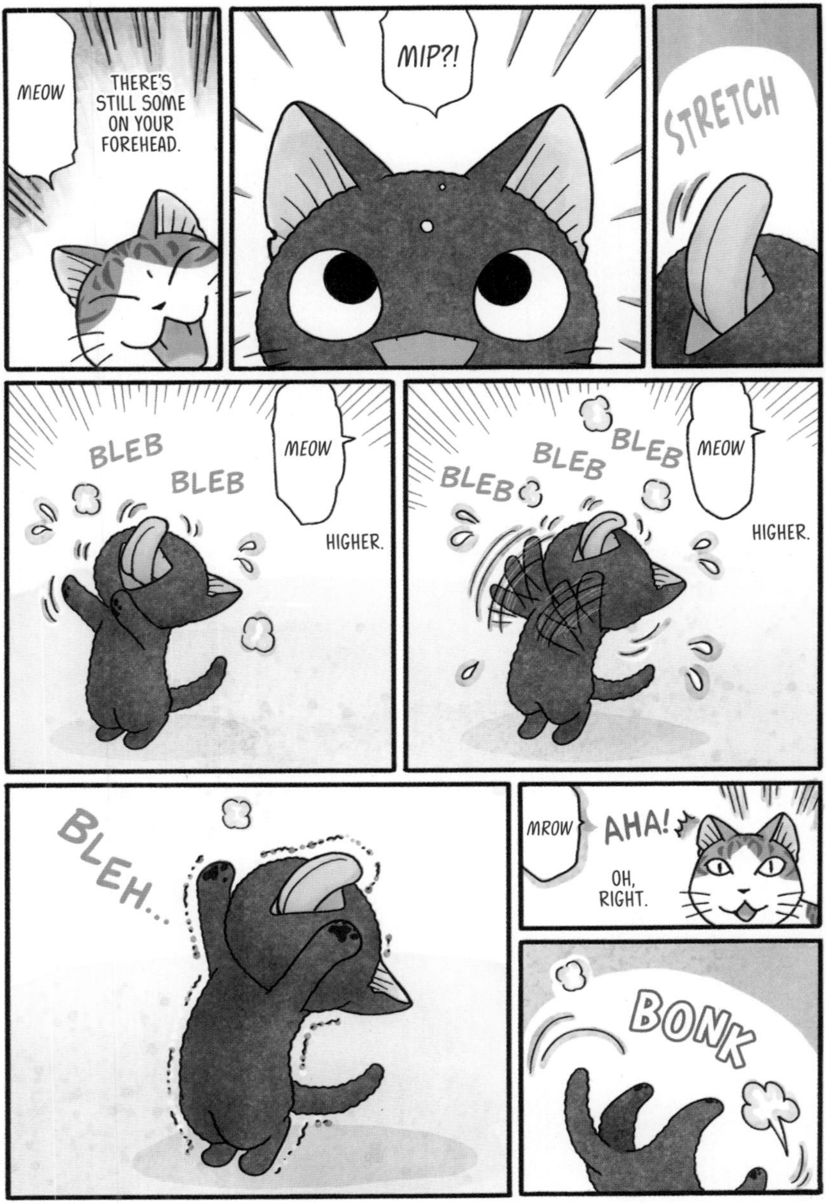
MEOW
THERE'S STILL SOME ON YOUR FOREHEAD.
MIP?!
STRETCH
BLEB
BLEB
MEOW
HIGHER.
BLEB
BLEB
BLEB
MEOW
HIGHER.
BLEH...
MROW
AHA!
OH, RIGHT.
BONK

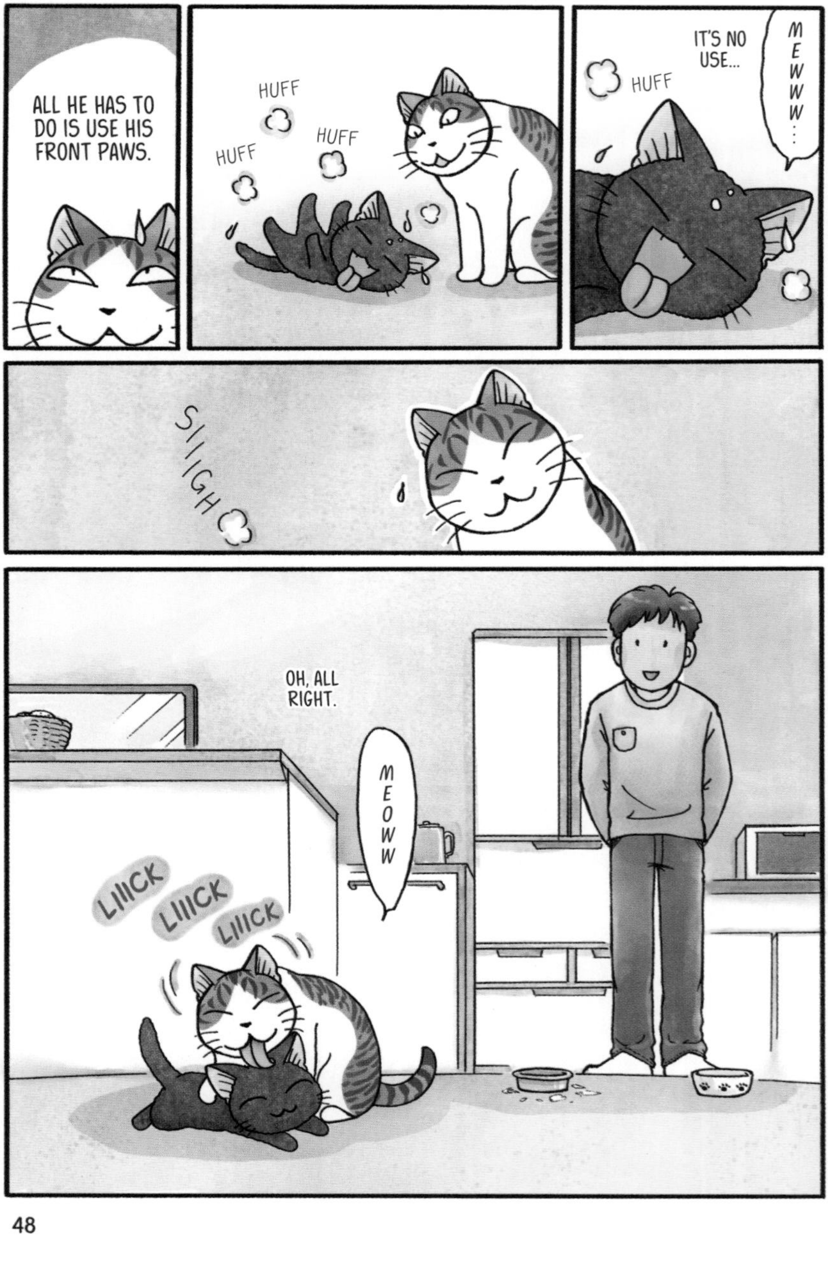
ALL HE HAS TO DO IS USE HIS FRONT PAWS.
HUFF
HUFF
HUFF
HUFF
IT'S NO USE...
MEWWWW...
SIIIGH
OH, ALL RIGHT.
MEOWW
LIIICK
LIIICK
LIIICK

CHAPTER 7 How to Play with Your Kitten

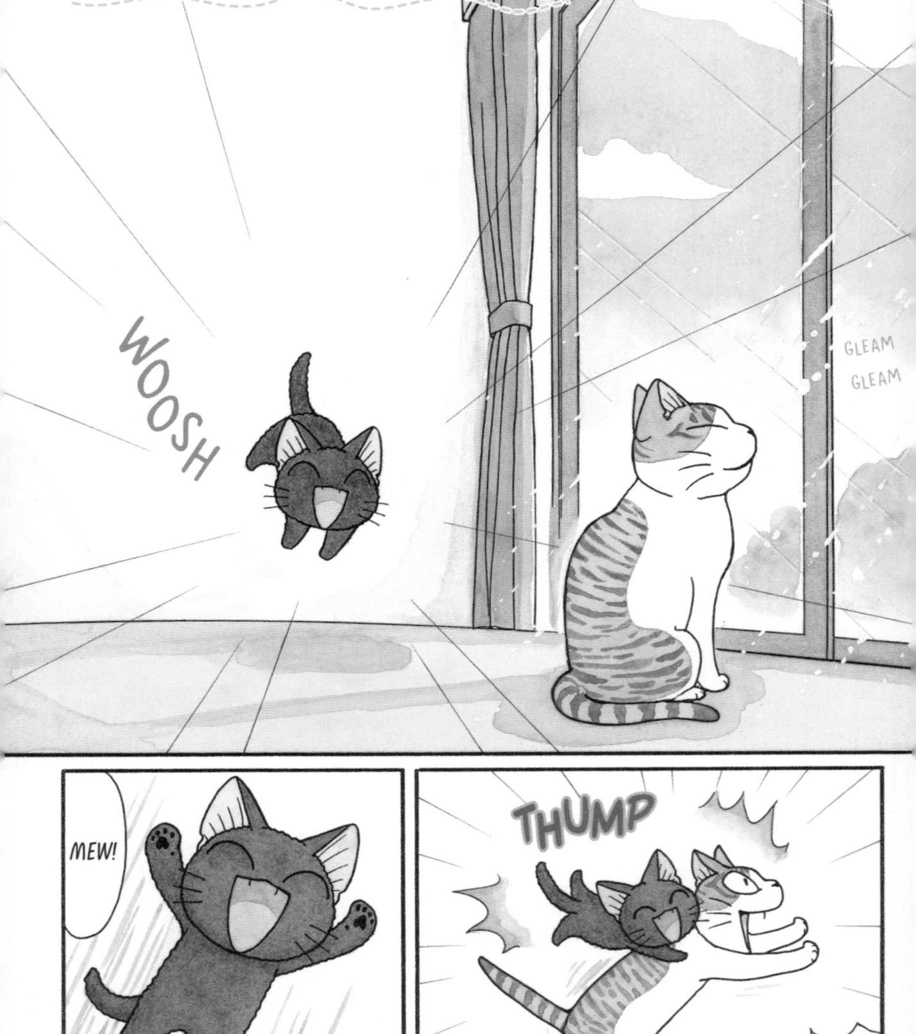
WOOSH
GLEAM
GLEAM
MEW!
TAK
THUMP
!

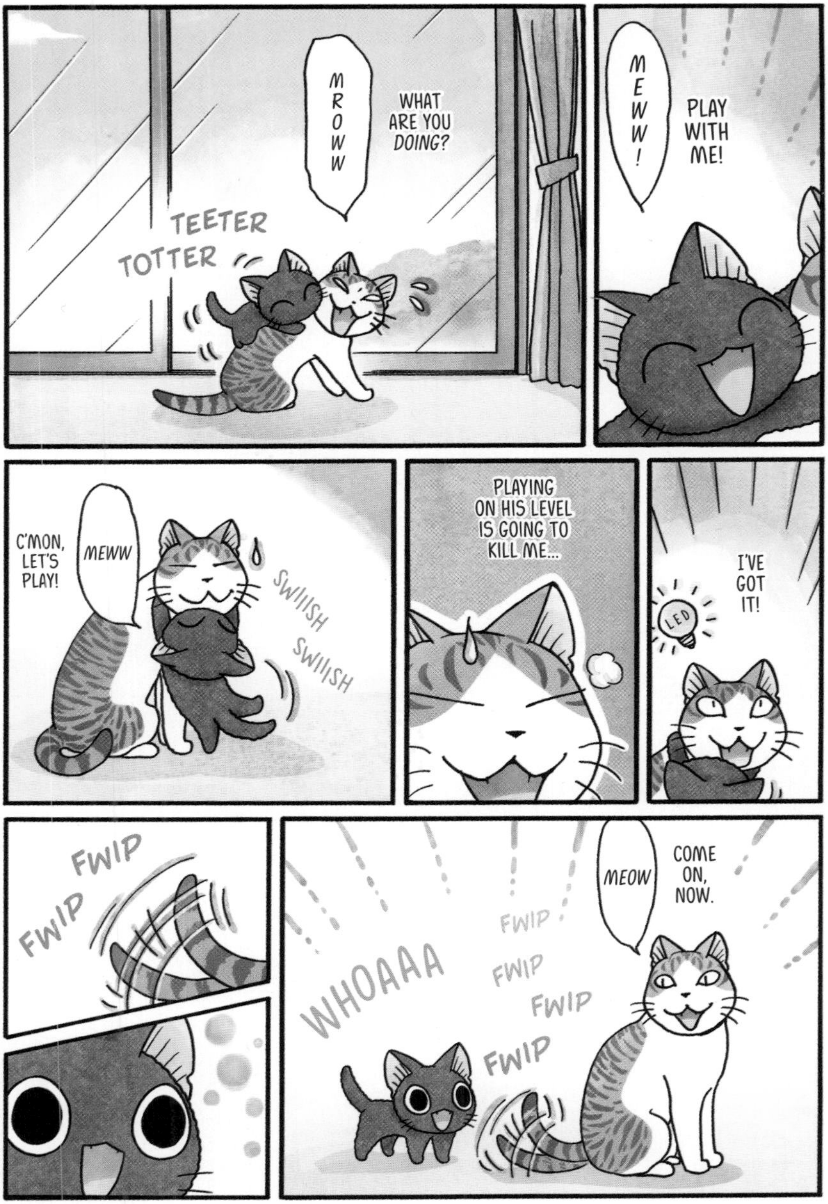
MROWW
WHAT ARE YOU DOING?
TEETER TOTTER
MEWW!
PLAY WITH ME!
C'MON, LET'S PLAY!
MEWW
SWIIISH
SWIIISH
PLAYING ON HIS LEVEL IS GOING TO KILL ME...
I'VE GOT IT!
LED
FWIP
FWIP
MEOW
COME ON, NOW.
WHOAAA
FWIP
FWIP
FWIP
FWIP

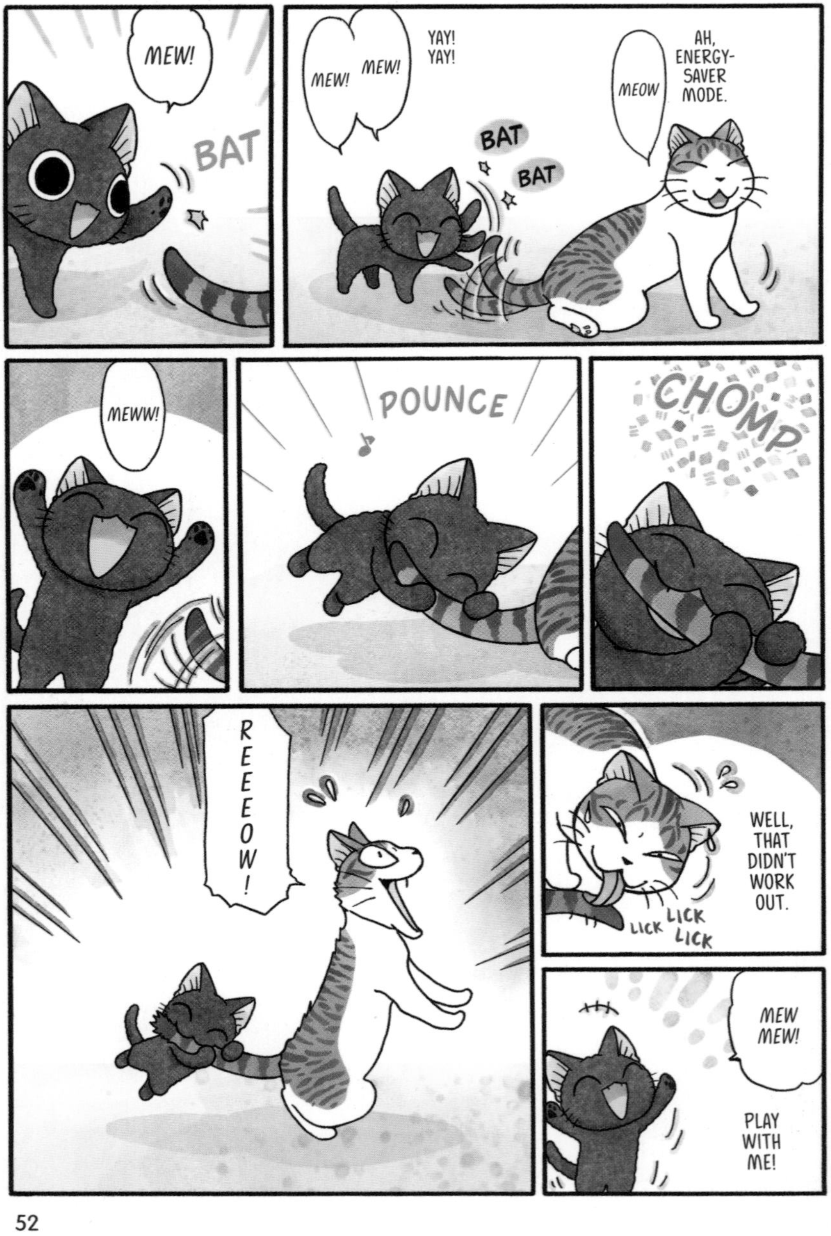
MEW!
BAT
MEW!
MEW!
YAY! YAY!
BAT
BAT
MEOW
AH, ENERGY-SAVER MODE.
MEWW!
POUNCE
CHOMP
REEEEOW!
WELL, THAT DIDN'T WORK OUT.
LICK
LICK
LICK
MEW MEW!
PLAY WITH ME!

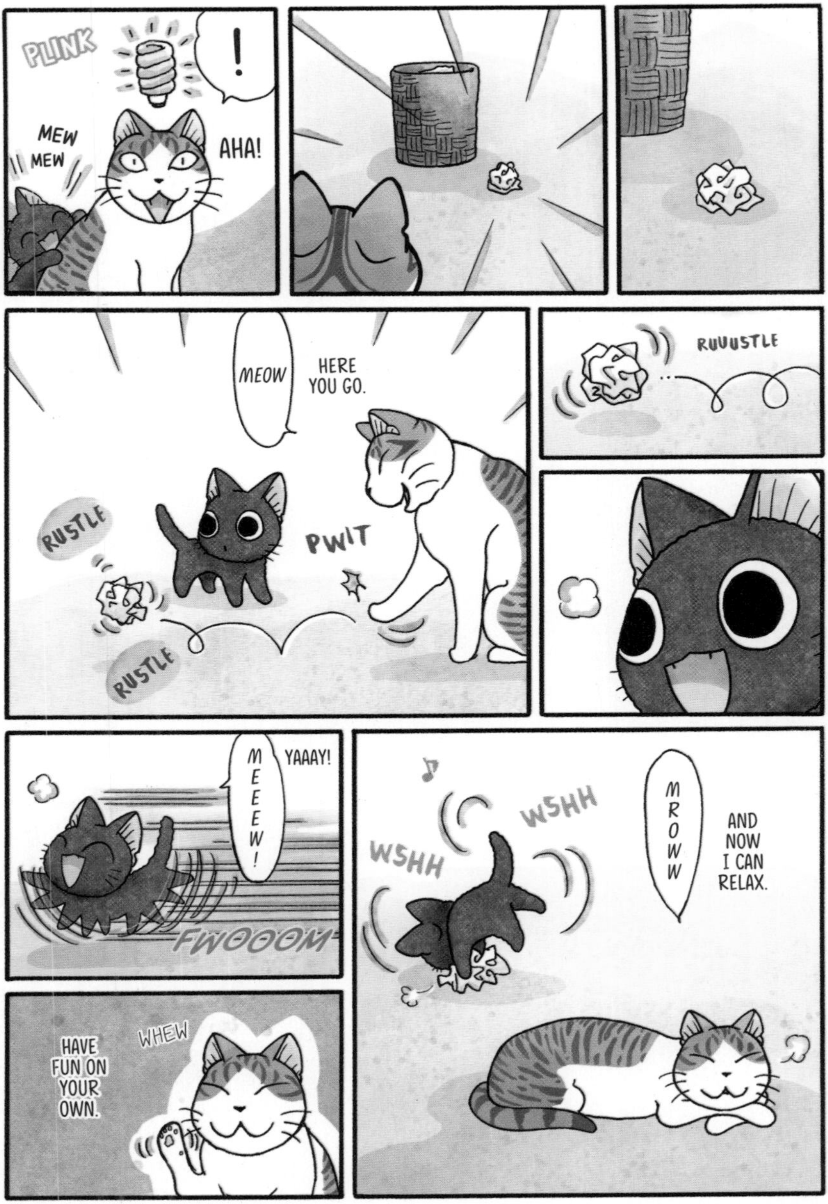
PLINK
!
MEW MEW
AHA!
MEOW
HERE YOU GO.
RUSTLE
PWIT
RUSTLE
RUUUSTLE
MEEEEW!
YAAAY!
FWOOOM
WHEW
HAVE FUN ON YOUR OWN.
MROWW
AND NOW I CAN RELAX.
WSHH
WSHH

WSHH

WSHH KSHH

PYOOM!

POUNCE

RUSTLE

SNAG

MEWW MEWW!

MEOW

OH, YOU'RE STUCK.

SIIIGH...

MEOWW

EVEN I'M AT A LOSS WHEN THAT HAPPENS.

BAT

BAT

FIP

AH! I'M FREE!

MEEP!

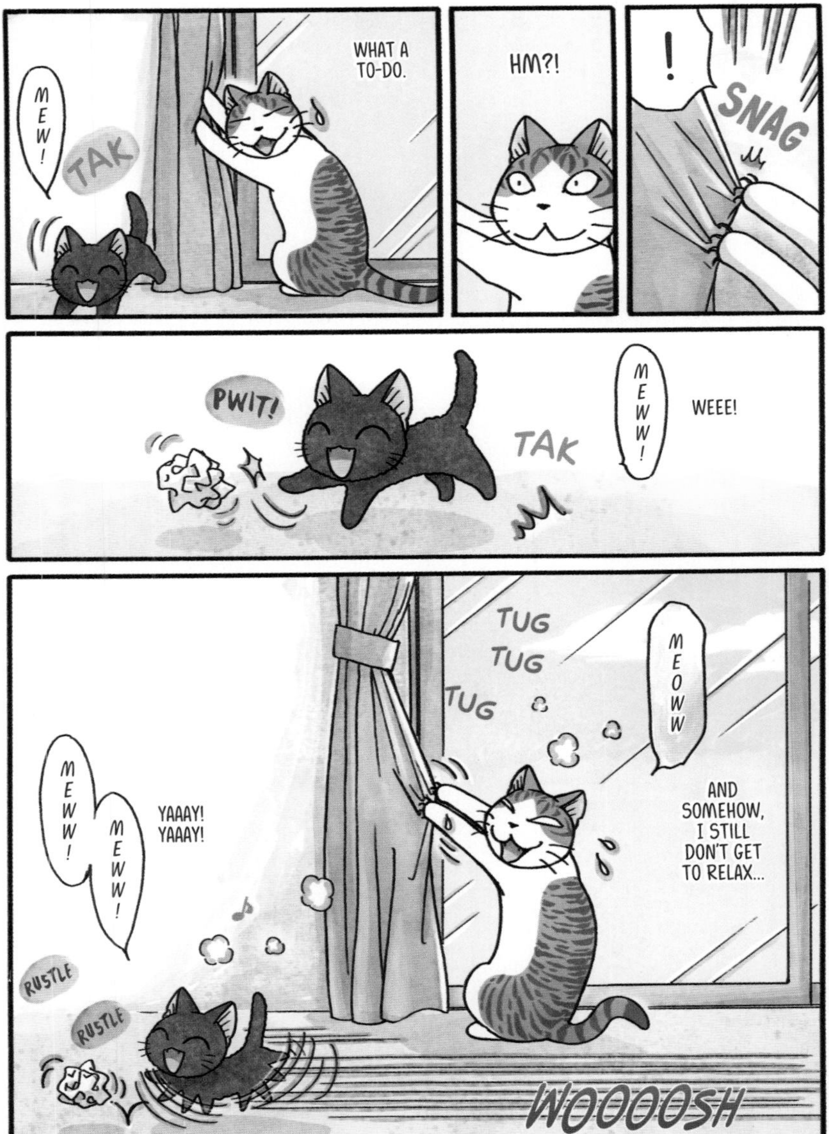

MEW!
TAK
WHAT A TO-DO.
HM?!
!
SNAG
PWIT!
TAK
MEWW!
WEEE!
MEWW!
MEWW!
YAAAY! YAAAY!
RUSTLE
RUSTLE
RUSTLE
TUG
TUG
TUG
MEOWW
AND SOMEHOW, I STILL DON'T GET TO RELAX...
WOOOOSH

Sue & Tai-chan

CHAPTER 8 But the *Other* Food...?!

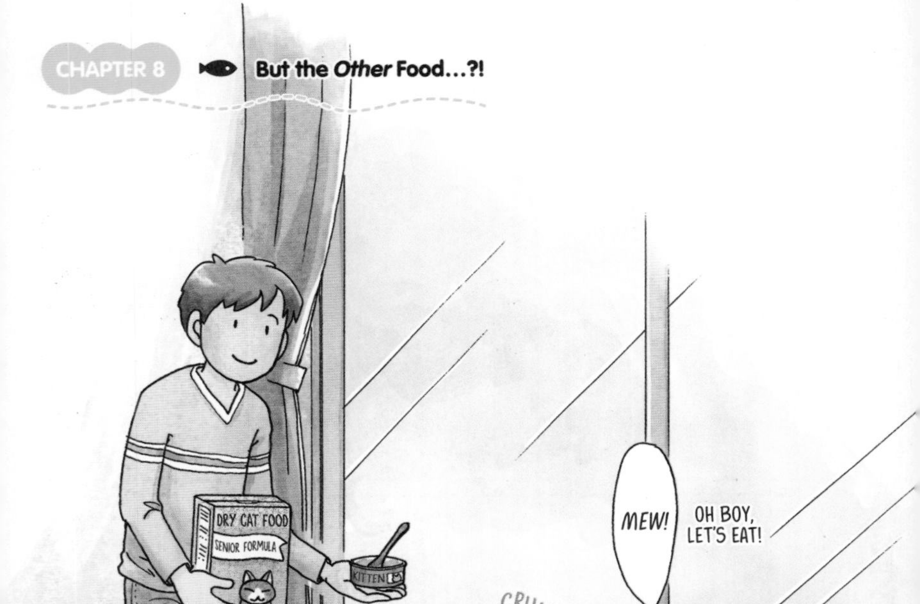
DRY CAT FOOD
SENIOR FORMULA
KITTEN
CRUNCH CRUNCH
MEW!
OH BOY, LET'S EAT!

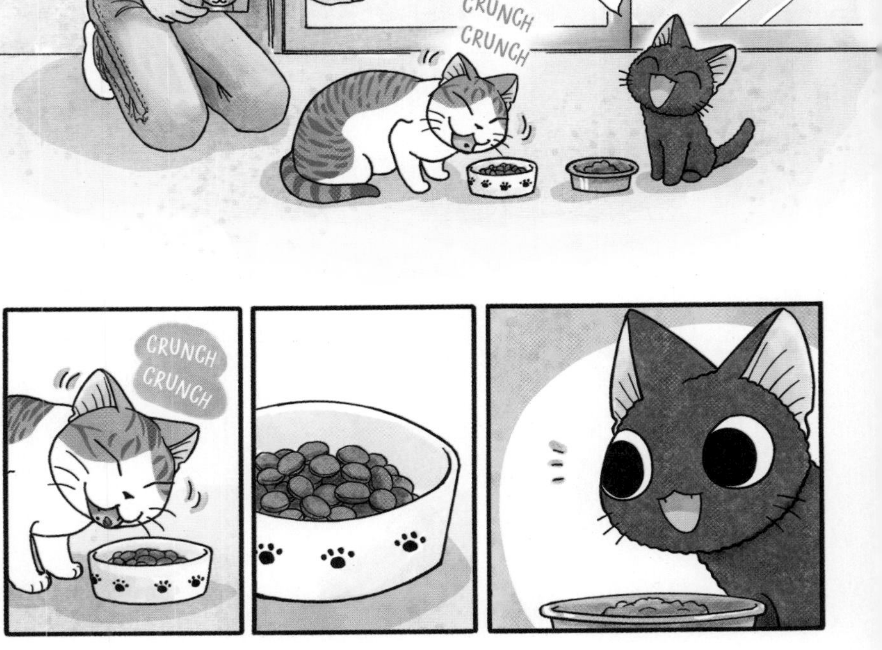
CRUNCH CRUNCH

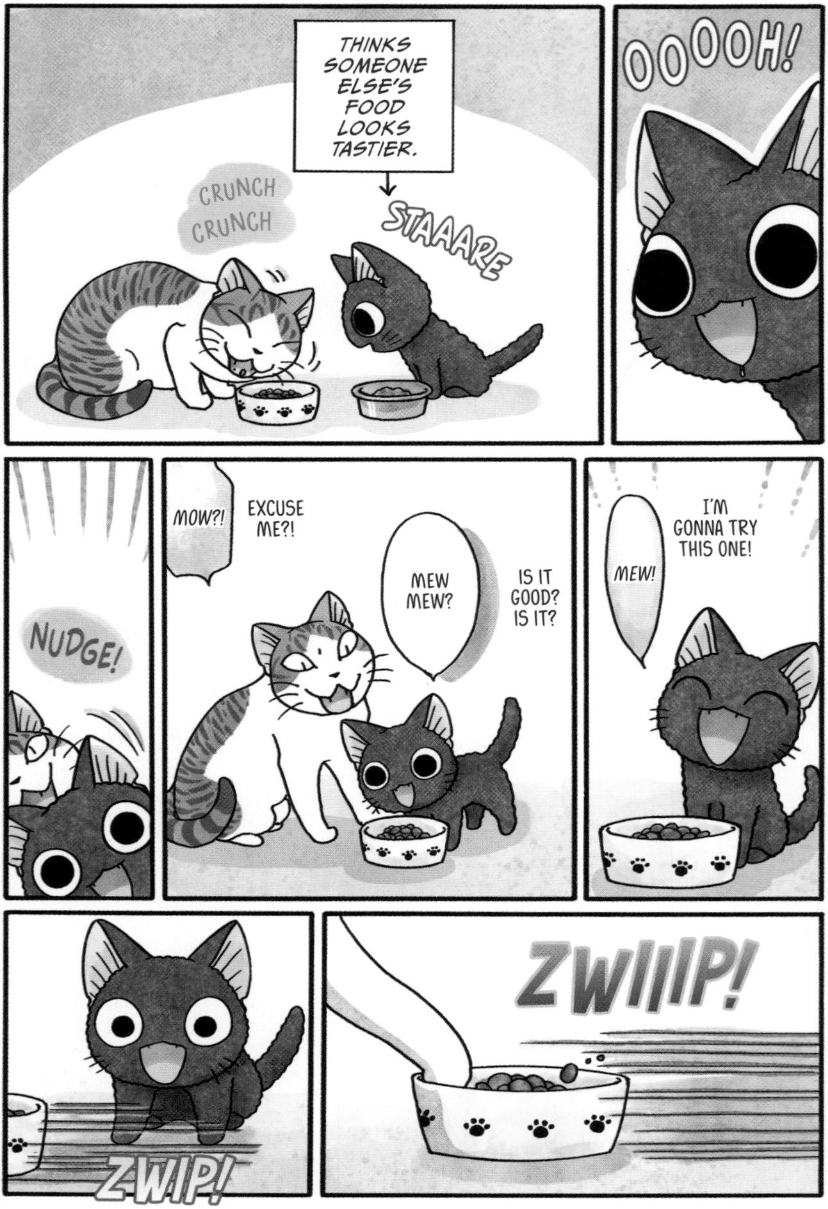
THINKS SOMEONE ELSE'S FOOD LOOKS TASTIER.
CRUNCH CRUNCH
STAAAARE
OOOOH!
NUDGE!
MOW?!
EXCUSE ME?!
MEW MEW?
IS IT GOOD? IS IT?
MEW!
I'M GONNA TRY THIS ONE!
ZWIP!
ZWIIIP!

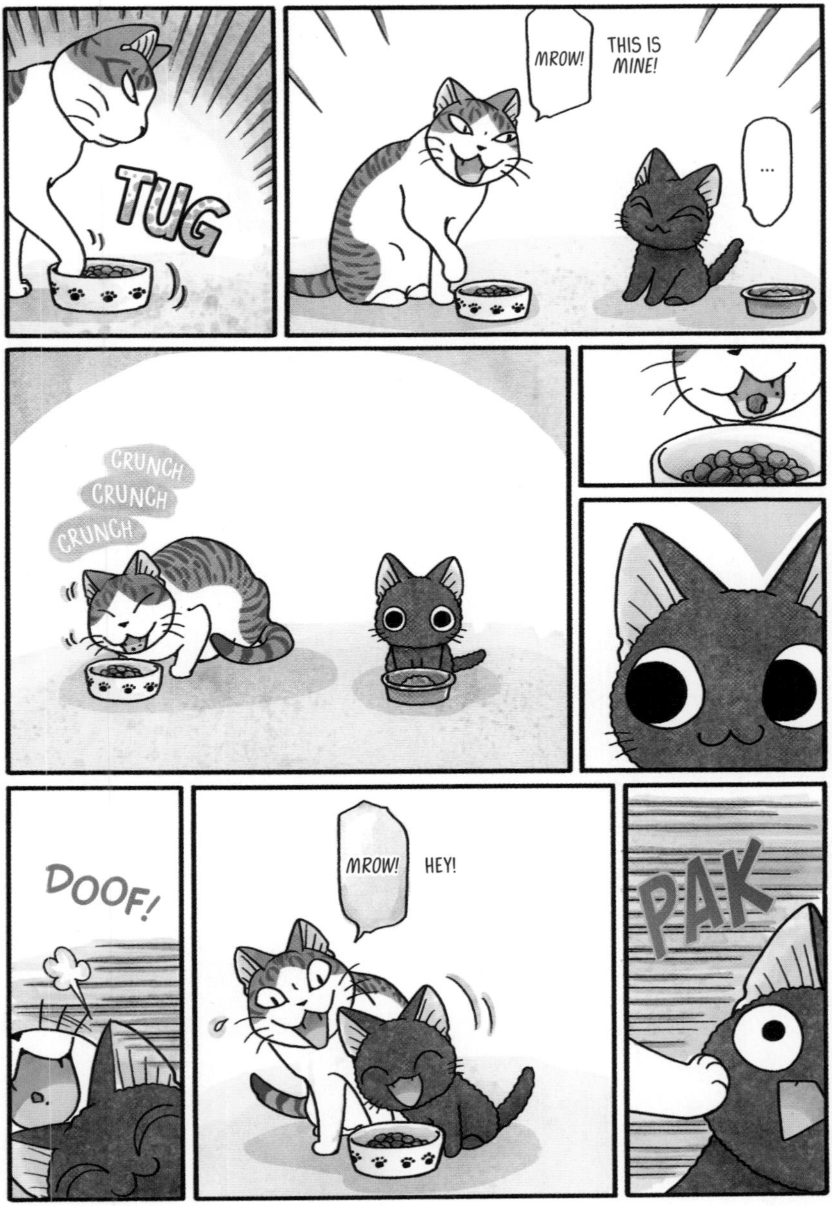

TUG
MROW!
THIS IS MINE!
...
CRUNCH
CRUNCH
CRUNCH
DOOF!
MROW!
HEY!
PAK

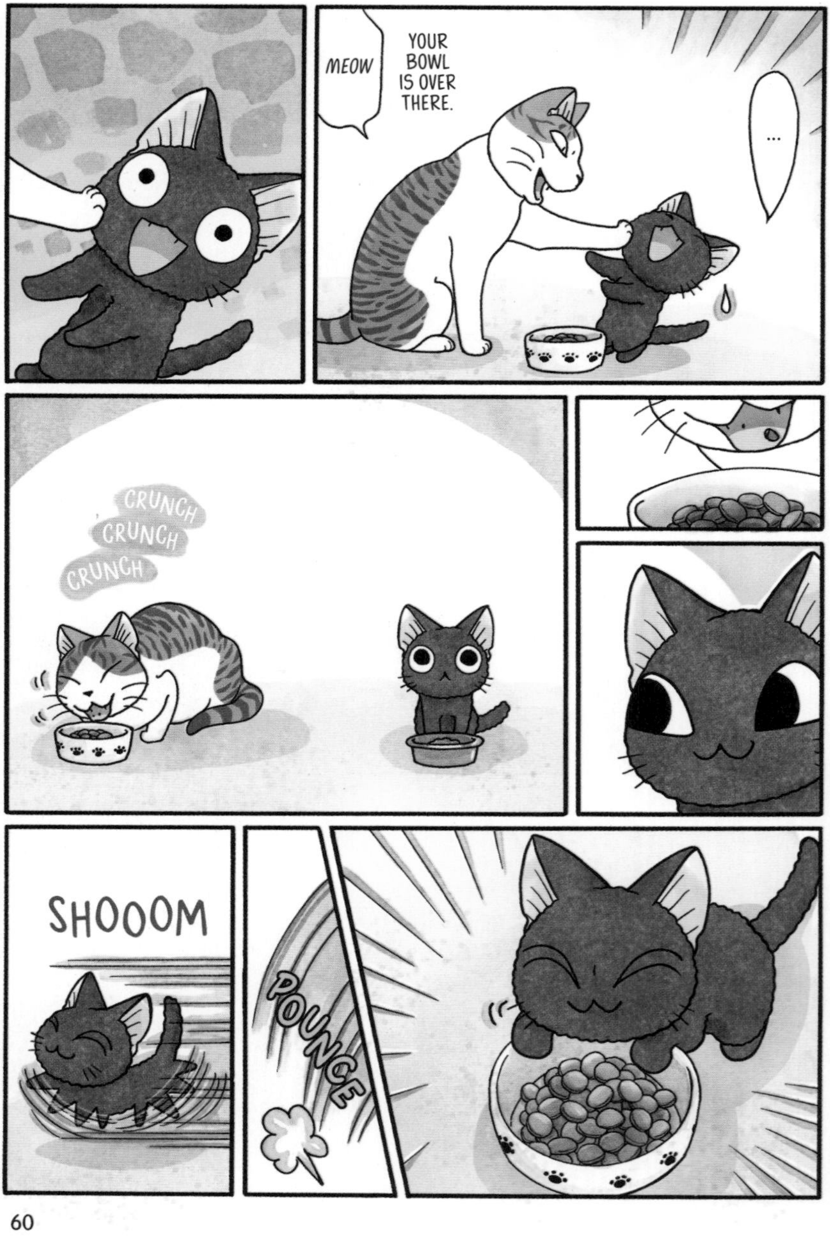

MEOW
YOUR BOWL IS OVER THERE.
...
CRUNCH
CRUNCH
CRUNCH
SHOOOM
POUNCE

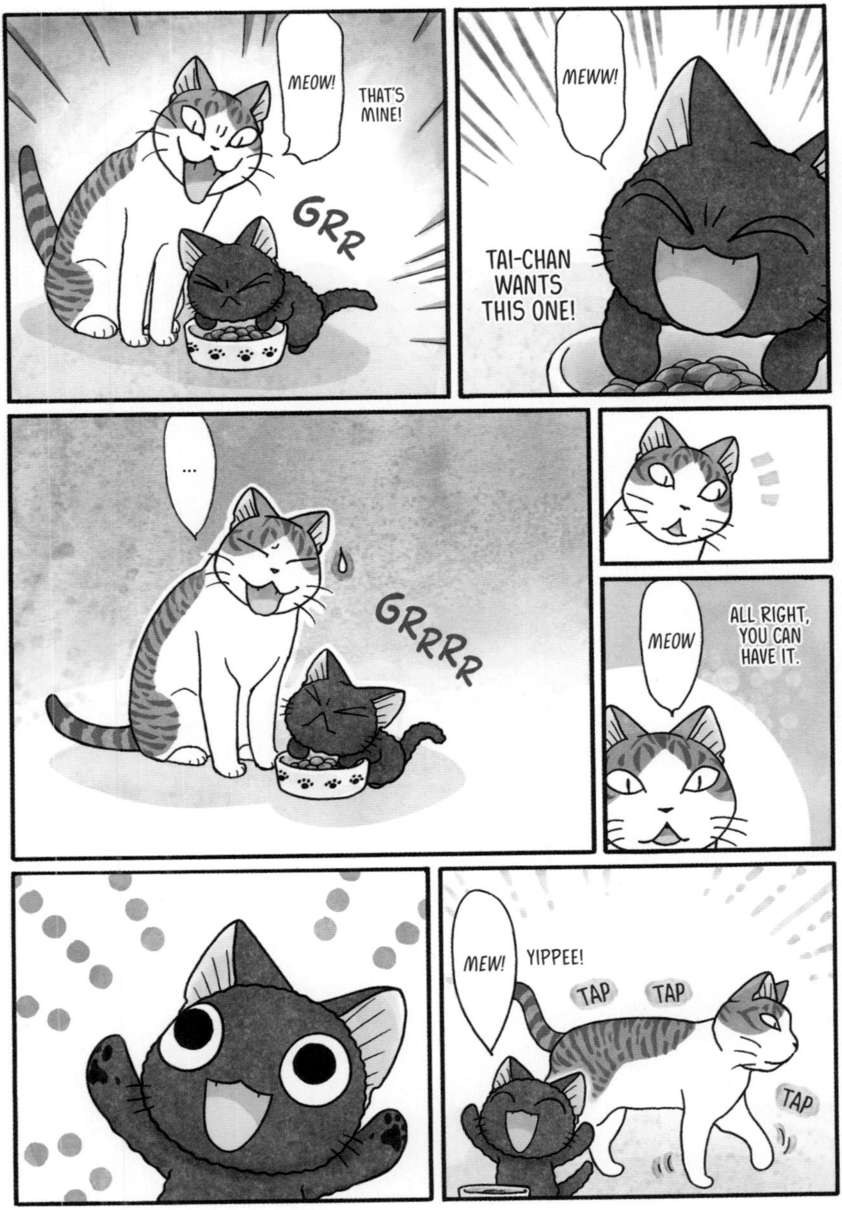

MEOW!
THAT'S MINE!
GRR
MEWW!
TAI-CHAN WANTS THIS ONE!
...
GRRRR
MEOW
ALL RIGHT, YOU CAN HAVE IT.
MEW!
YIPPEE!
TAP
TAP
TAP

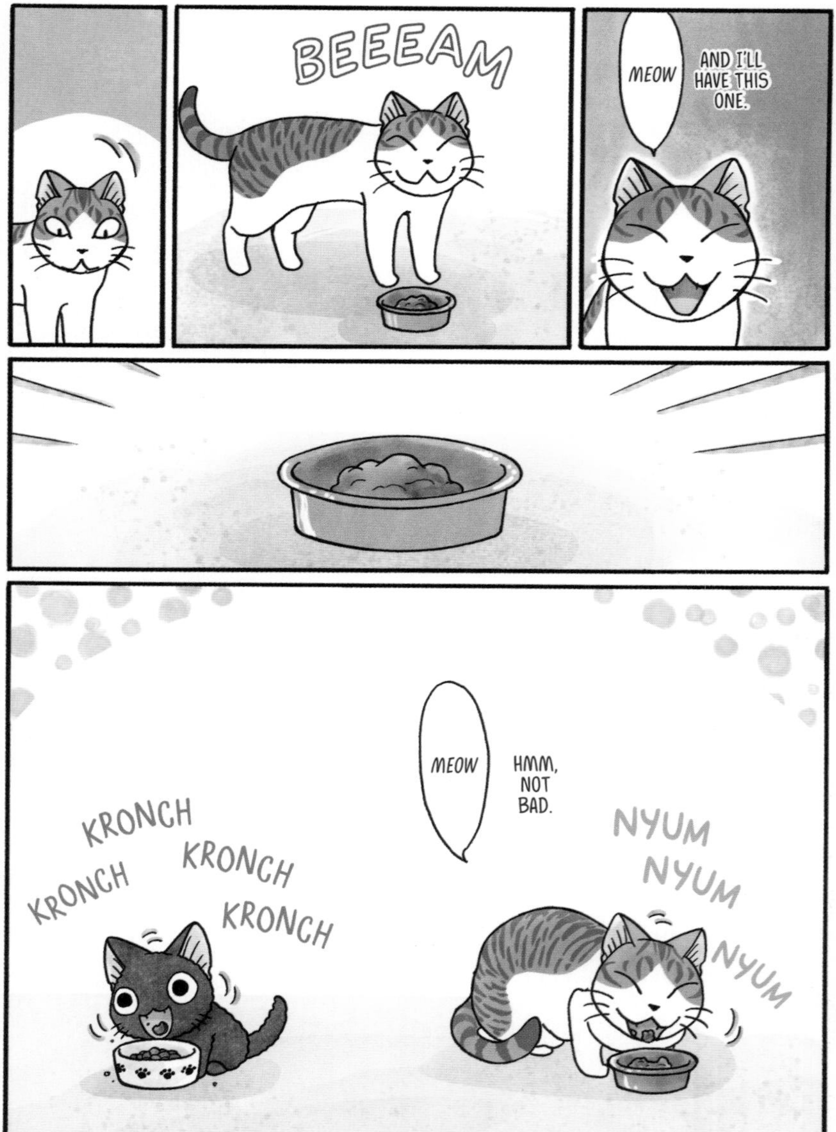
BEEEAM
MEOW
AND I'LL HAVE THIS ONE.
KRONCH
KRONCH
KRONCH
KRONCH
MEOW
HMM, NOT BAD.
NYUM
NYUM
NYUM

CHAPTER 9 Cats at Midnight

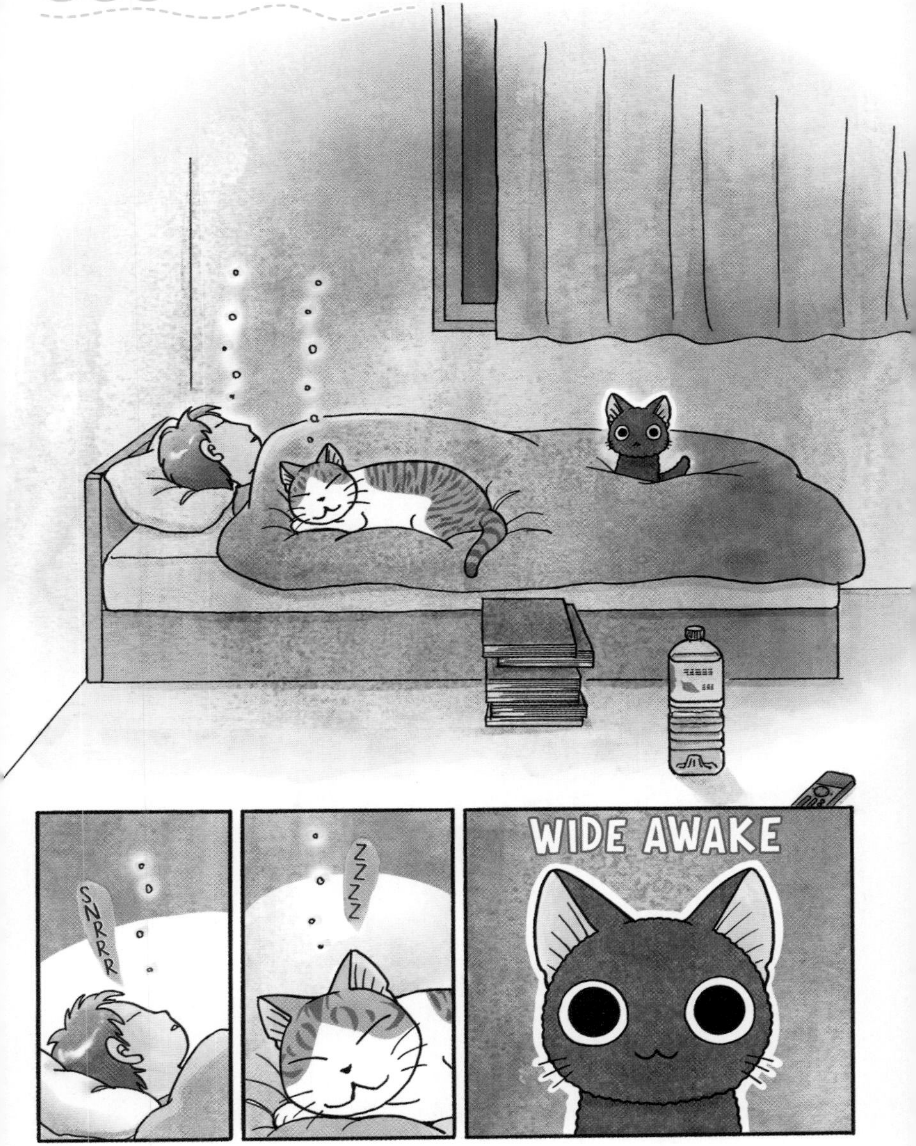
SNRRR
ZZZ
WIDE AWAKE

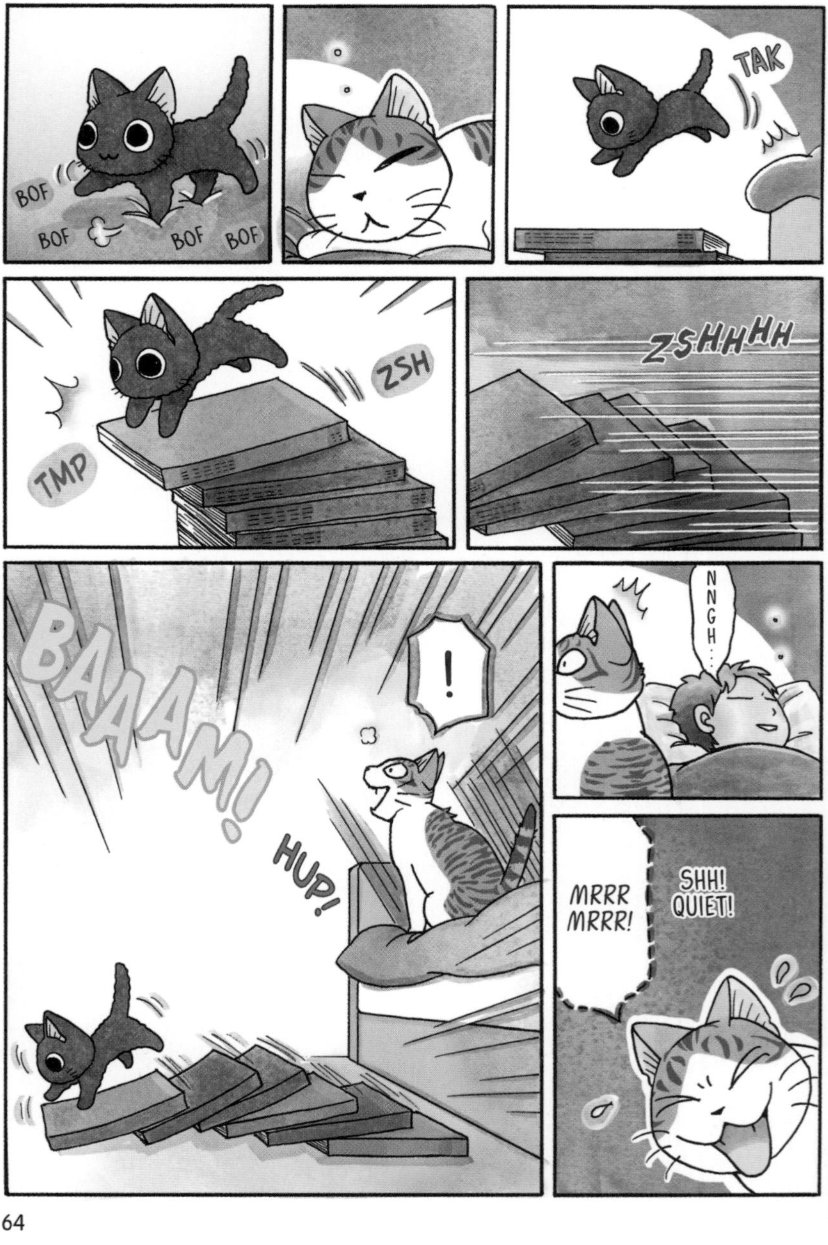
BOF
BOF
BOF
BOF
TAK
ZSH
TMP
ZSHHHHH
BAAAM!
!
HUP!
NNGH...
MRRR MRRR!
SHH! QUIET!

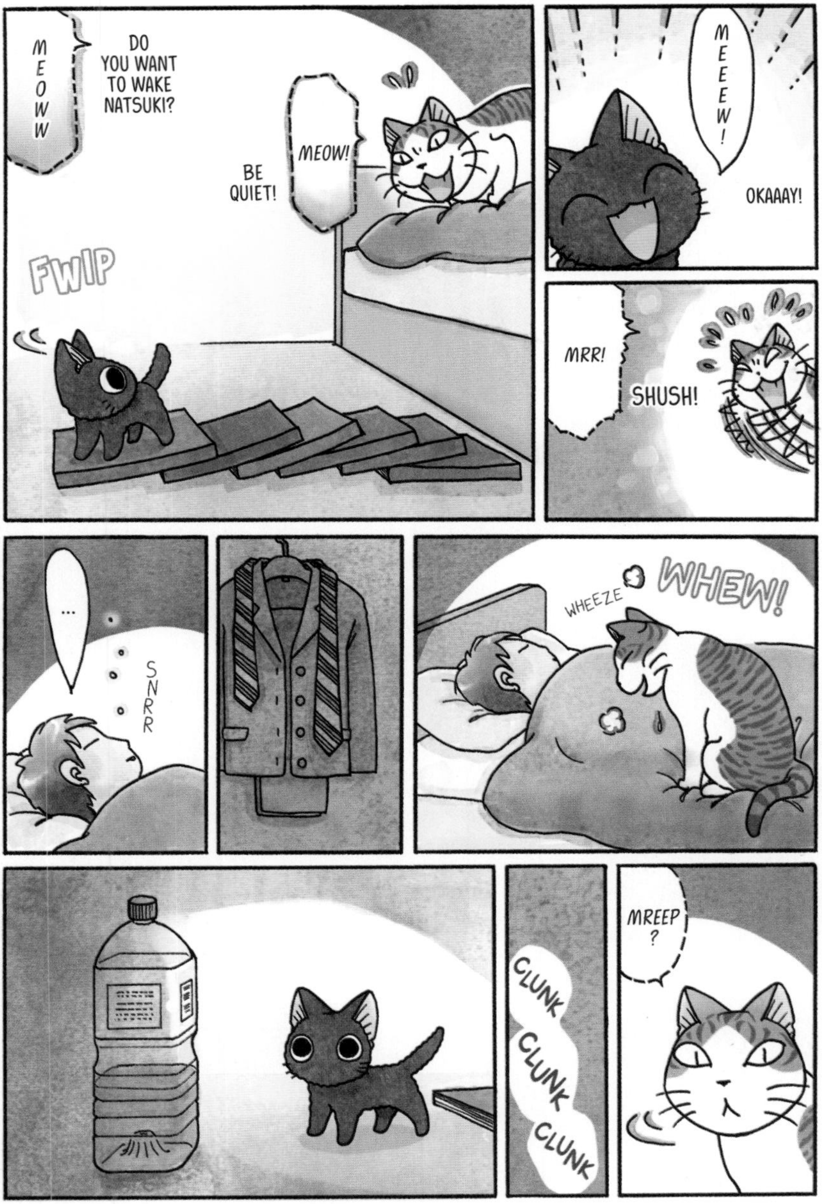
MEOWW
DO YOU WANT TO WAKE NATSUKI?
MEOW!
BE QUIET!
FWIP
MEEEEW!
OKAAAY!
MRR!
SHUSH!
...
SNRR
WHEEZE
WHEW!
CLUNK
CLUNK
CLUNK
MREEP?

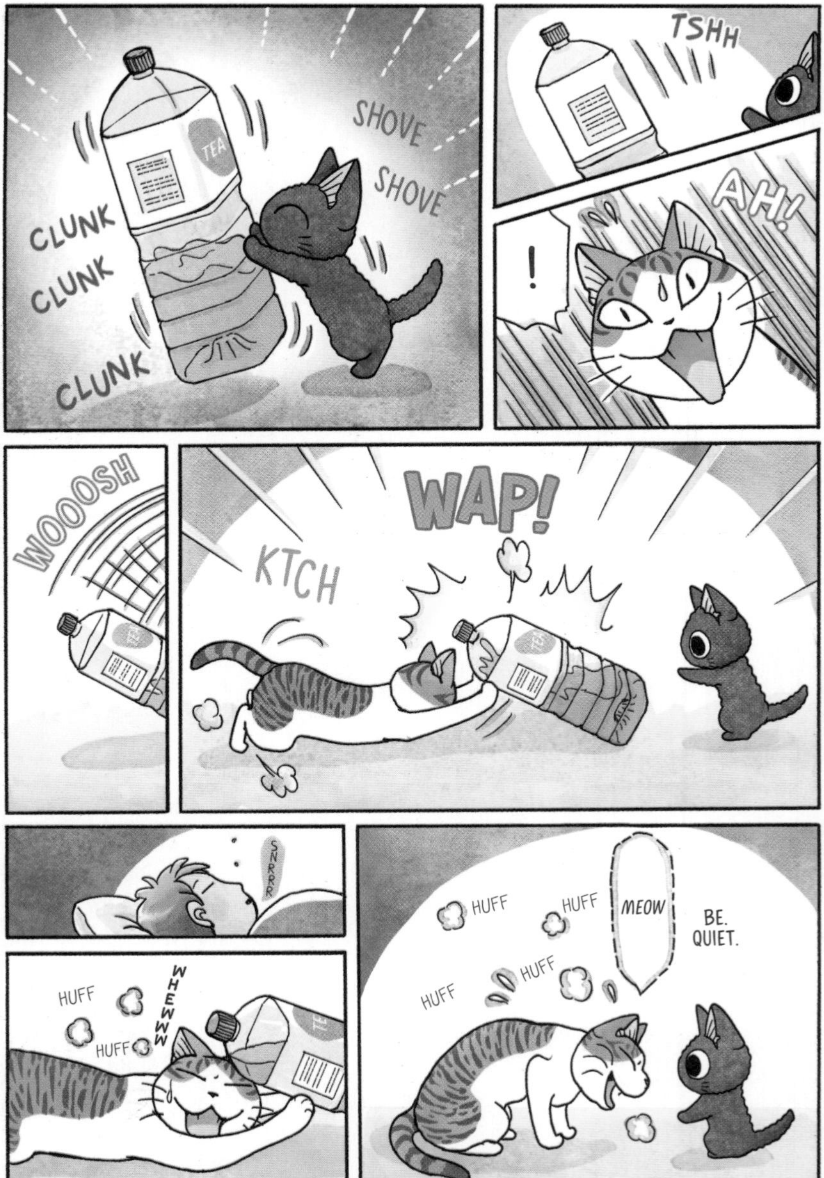
SHOVE
SHOVE
CLUNK
CLUNK
CLUNK
TSHH
AH!
!
WOOOSH
WAP!
KTCH
SNRRR
HUFF
WHEWWW
HUFF
HUFF
HUFF
MEOW
BE. QUIET.
HUFF
HUFF

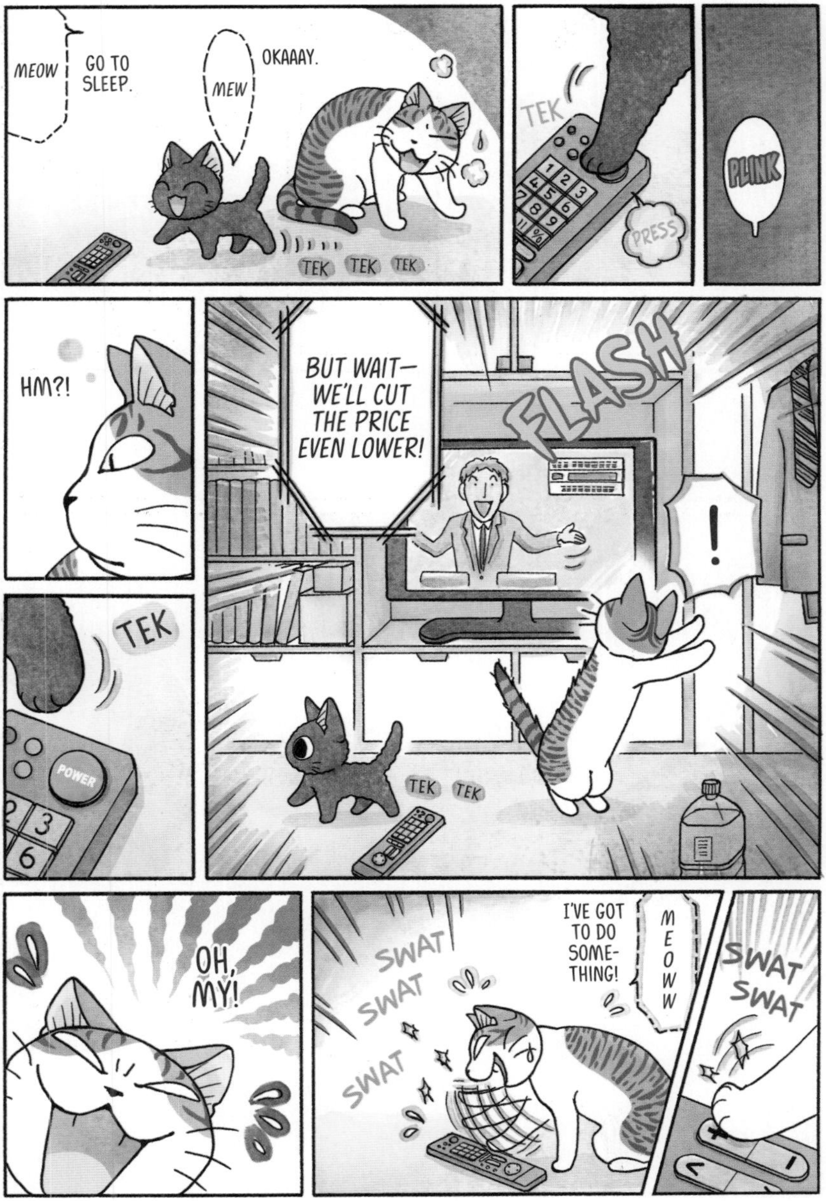
MEOW
GO TO SLEEP.
MEW
OKAAAY.
TEK TEK TEK
TEK
PRESS
PLINK
HM?!
BUT WAIT— WE'LL CUT THE PRICE EVEN LOWER!
FLASH
!
TEK TEK
TEK
POWER
OH, MY!
SWAT SWAT SWAT
I'VE GOT TO DO SOME-THING!
MEOWW
SWAT SWAT

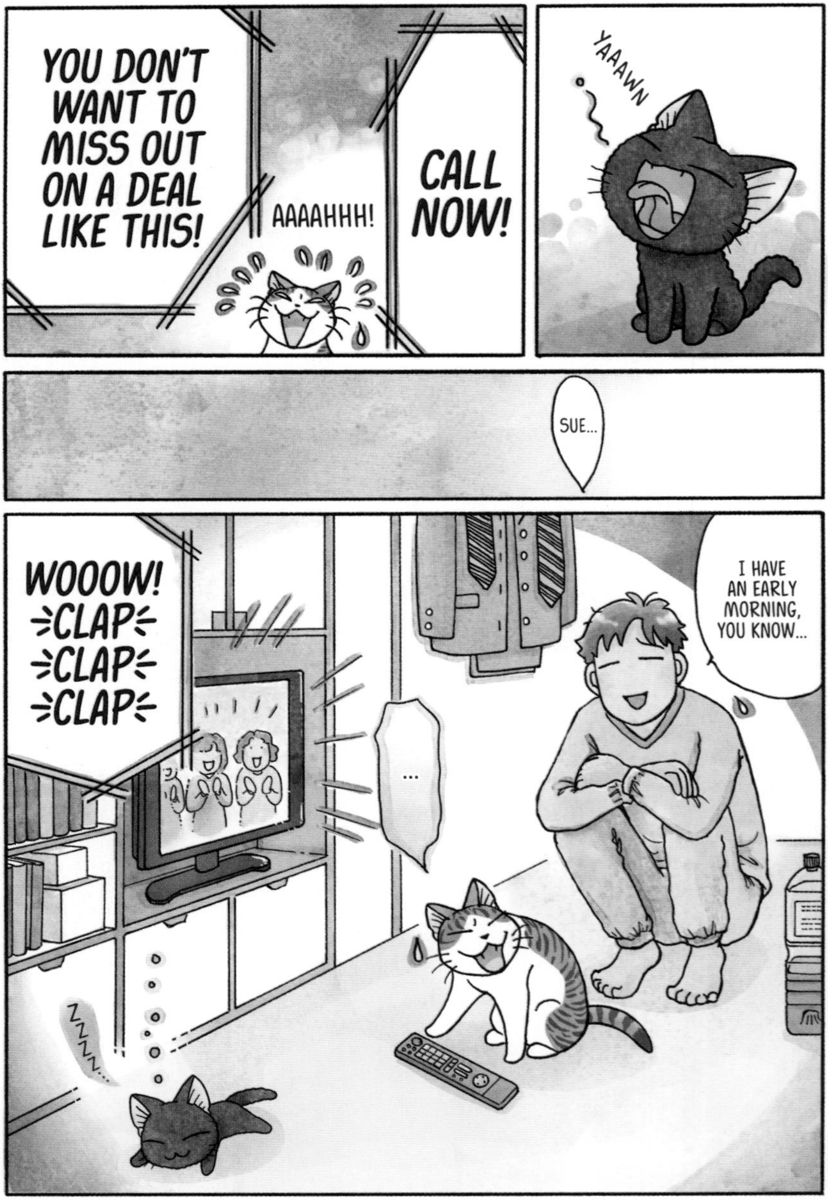
YOU DON'T WANT TO MISS OUT ON A DEAL LIKE THIS!
AAAAHHH!
CALL NOW!
YAAAWN
SUE...
WOOOW! CLAP CLAP CLAP
...
I HAVE AN EARLY MORNING, YOU KNOW...
ZZZZ...

Sue & Tai-chan

CHAPTER 10 Where the Good Water Is

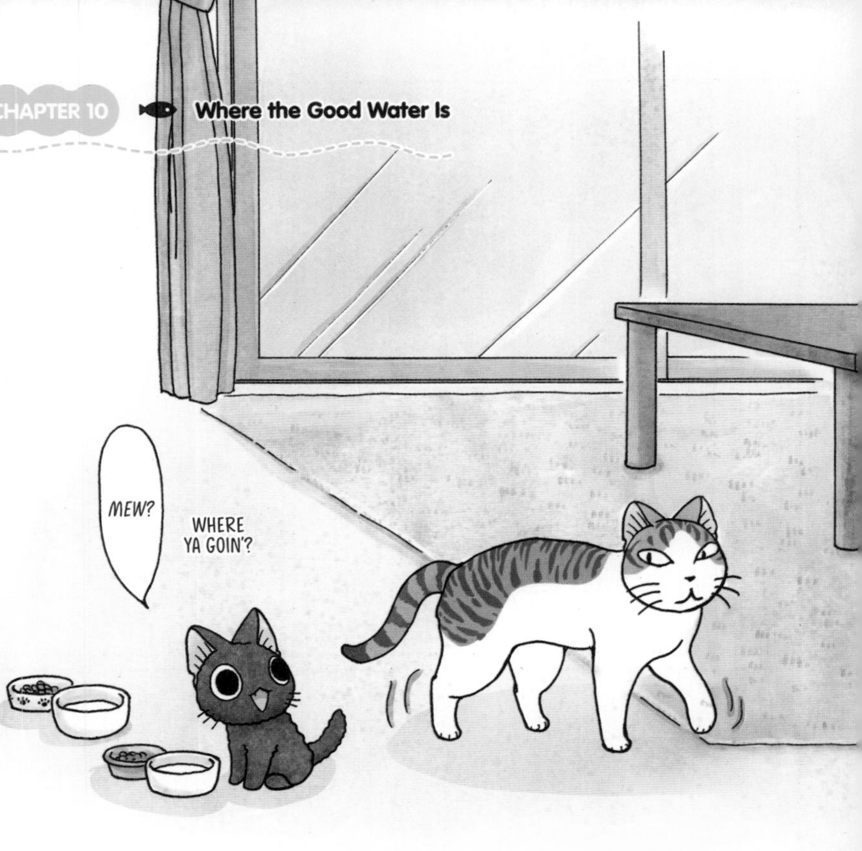
MEW?
WHERE YA GOIN'?

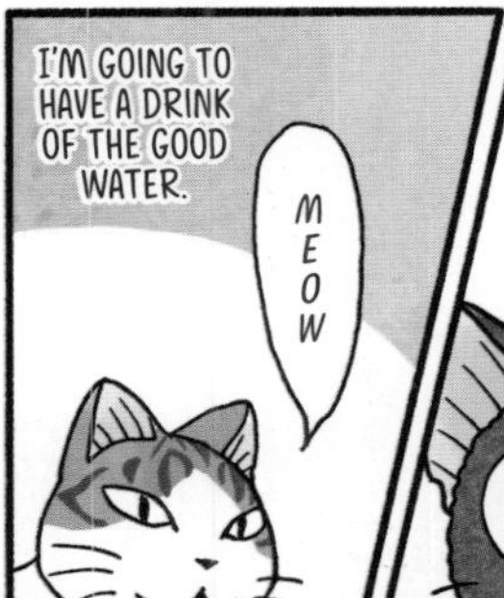
I'M GOING TO HAVE A DRINK OF THE GOOD WATER.
MEOW

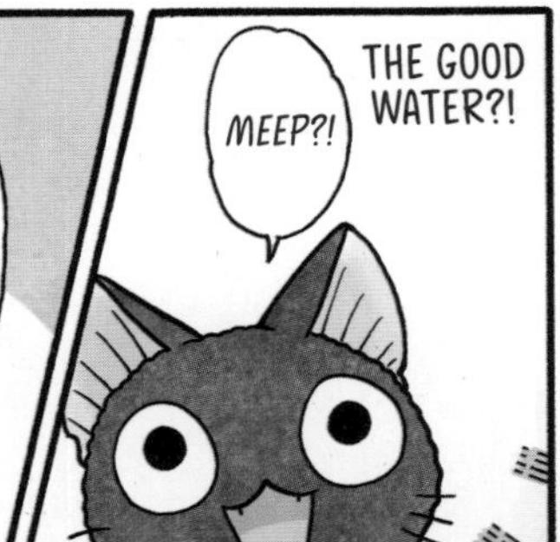
MEEP?!
THE GOOD WATER?!

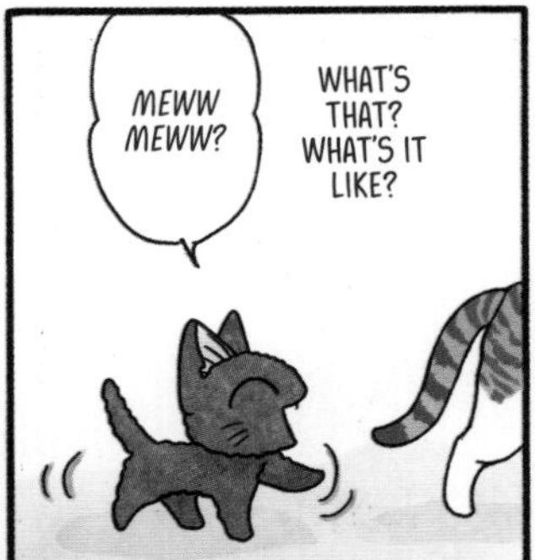
MEWW MEWW?
WHAT'S THAT? WHAT'S IT LIKE?
TEK TEK TEK

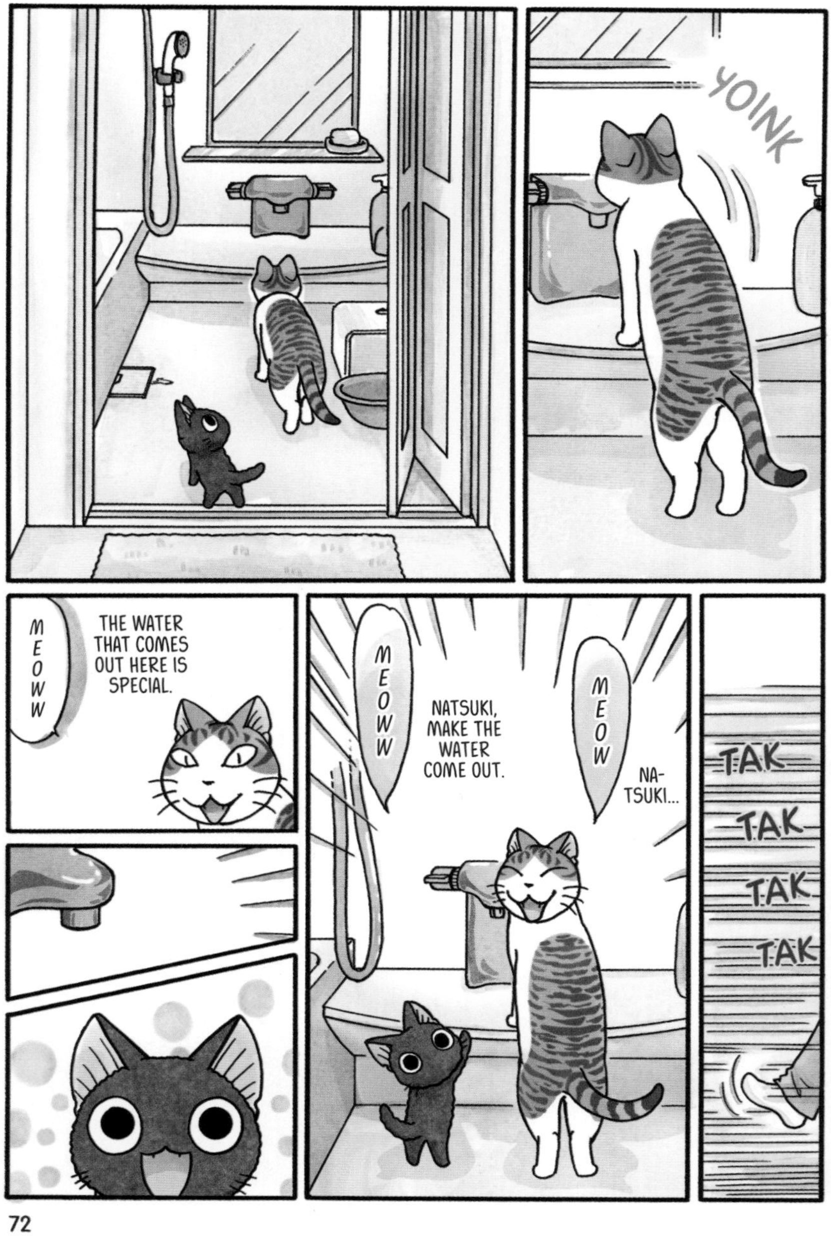
YOINK
MEOWW
THE WATER THAT COMES OUT HERE IS SPECIAL.
MEOWW
NATSUKI, MAKE THE WATER COME OUT.
MEOW
NA-TSUKI...
TAK
TAK
TAK
TAK

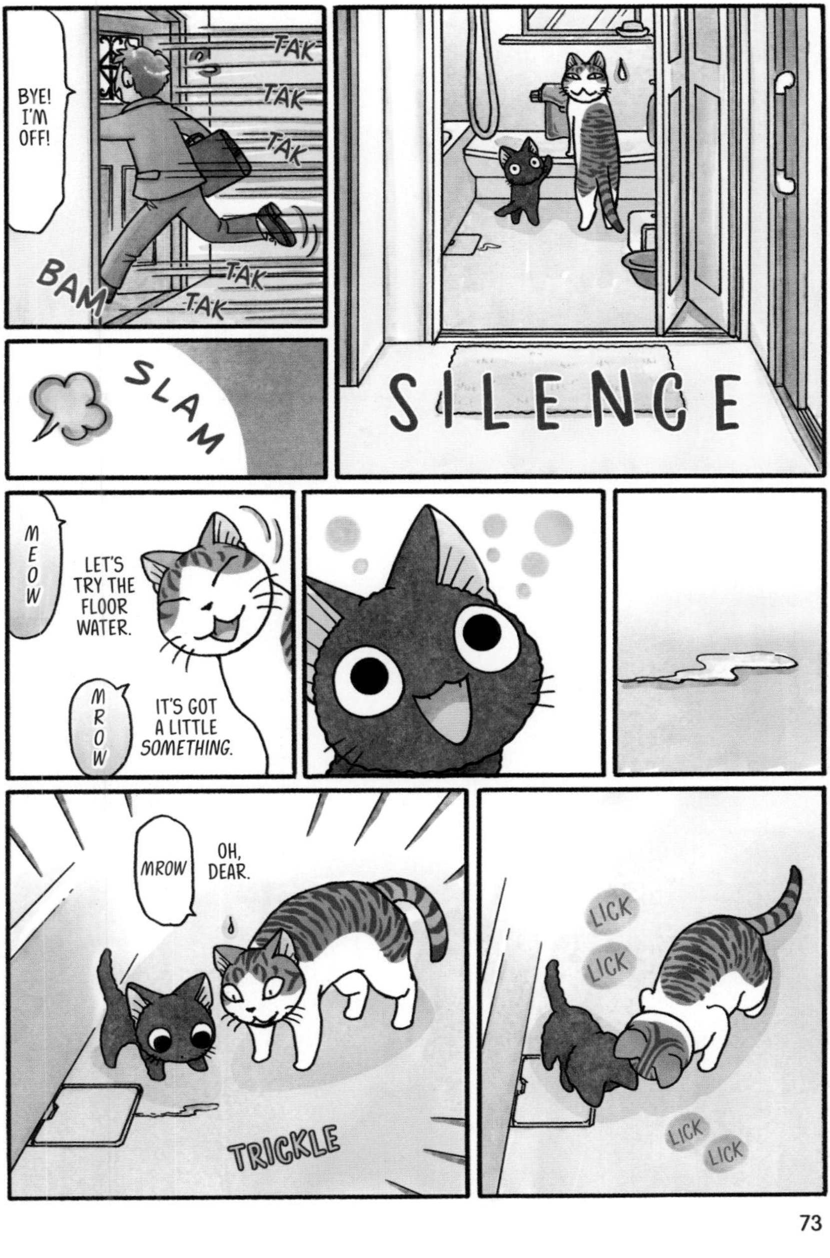
BYE! I'M OFF!
TAK
TAK
TAK
TAK
TAK
BAM
SLAM
SILENCE
MEOW
LET'S TRY THE FLOOR WATER.
MROW
IT'S GOT A LITTLE SOMETHING.
MROW
OH, DEAR.
TRICKLE
LICK
LICK
LICK
LICK

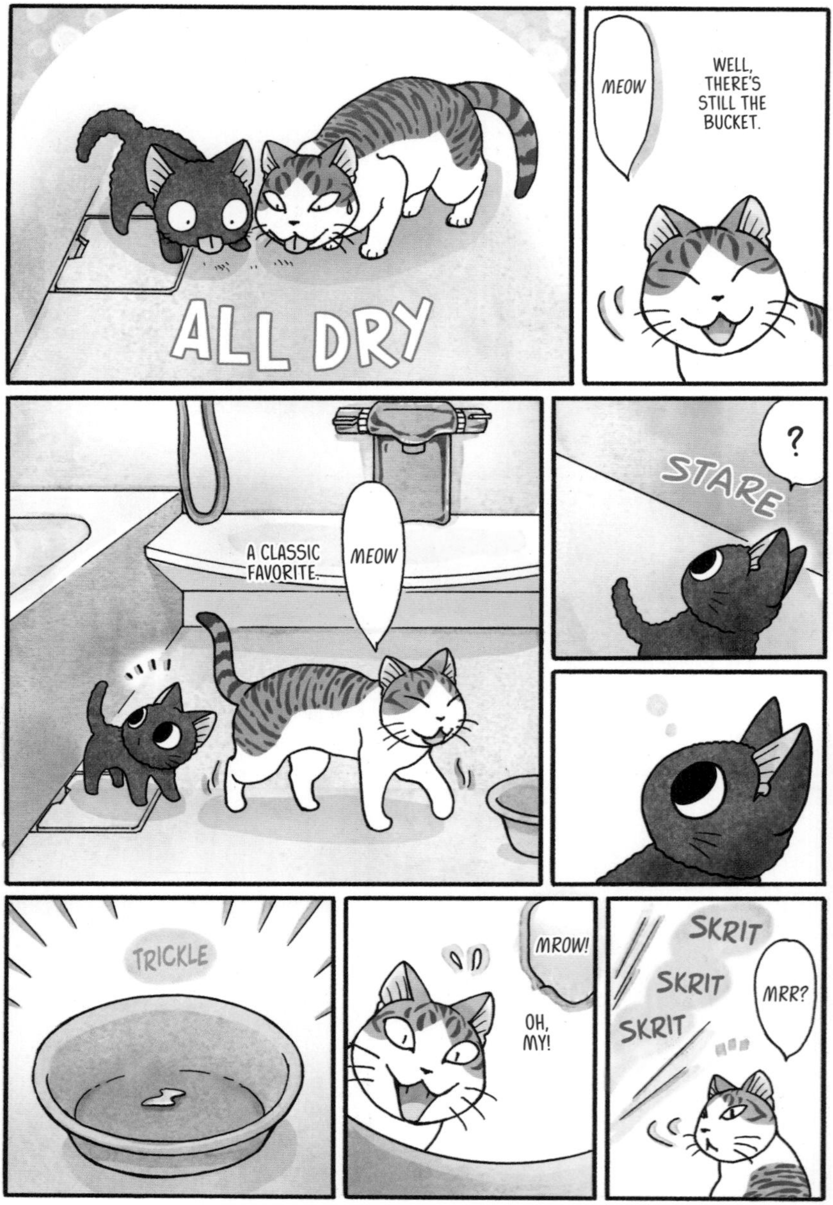
ALL DRY
MEOW
WELL, THERE'S STILL THE BUCKET.
A CLASSIC FAVORITE.
MEOW
?
STARE
TRICKLE
MROW!
OH, MY!
SKRIT
SKRIT
SKRIT
MRR?

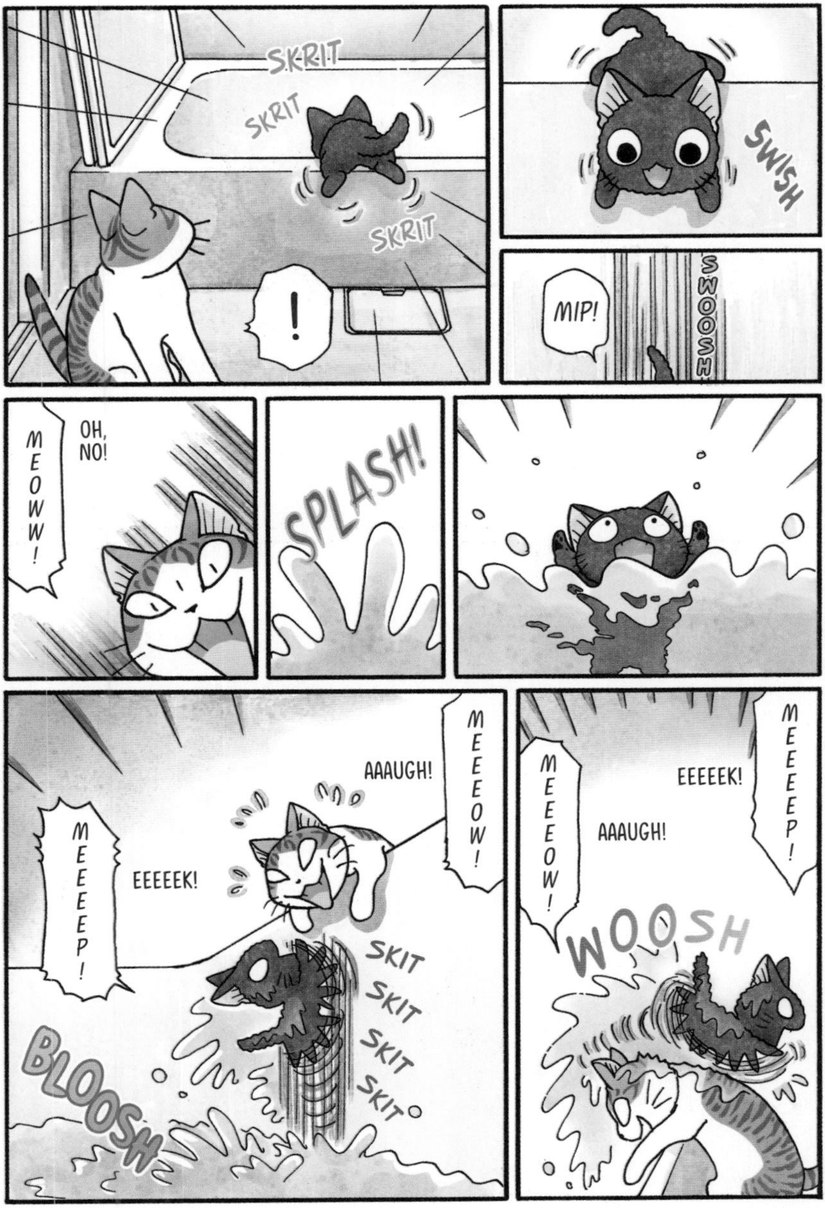
SKRIT
SKRIT
SKRIT
!
SWISH
MIP!
SWOOSH
OH, NO!
MEOWW!
SPLASH!
MEEEEP!
EEEEEK!
AAAUGH!
MEEEOW!
SKIT
SKIT
SKIT
SKIT
BLOOSH
MEEEOW!
AAAUGH!
EEEEEK!
MEEEEP!
WOOSH

MEEEP!

WOOSH

MROWW!

HUFF

HUFF

HUFF

HUFF

LICK LICK LICK LICK MLICK MLICK

HEY...

MIP

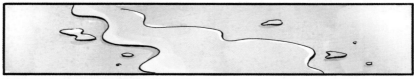

MEWW?

IS THIS WATER GOOD, TOO?

...MROW

...N-NO. NOT GOOD AT ALL.

CHAPTER 11 Still as a Statue...

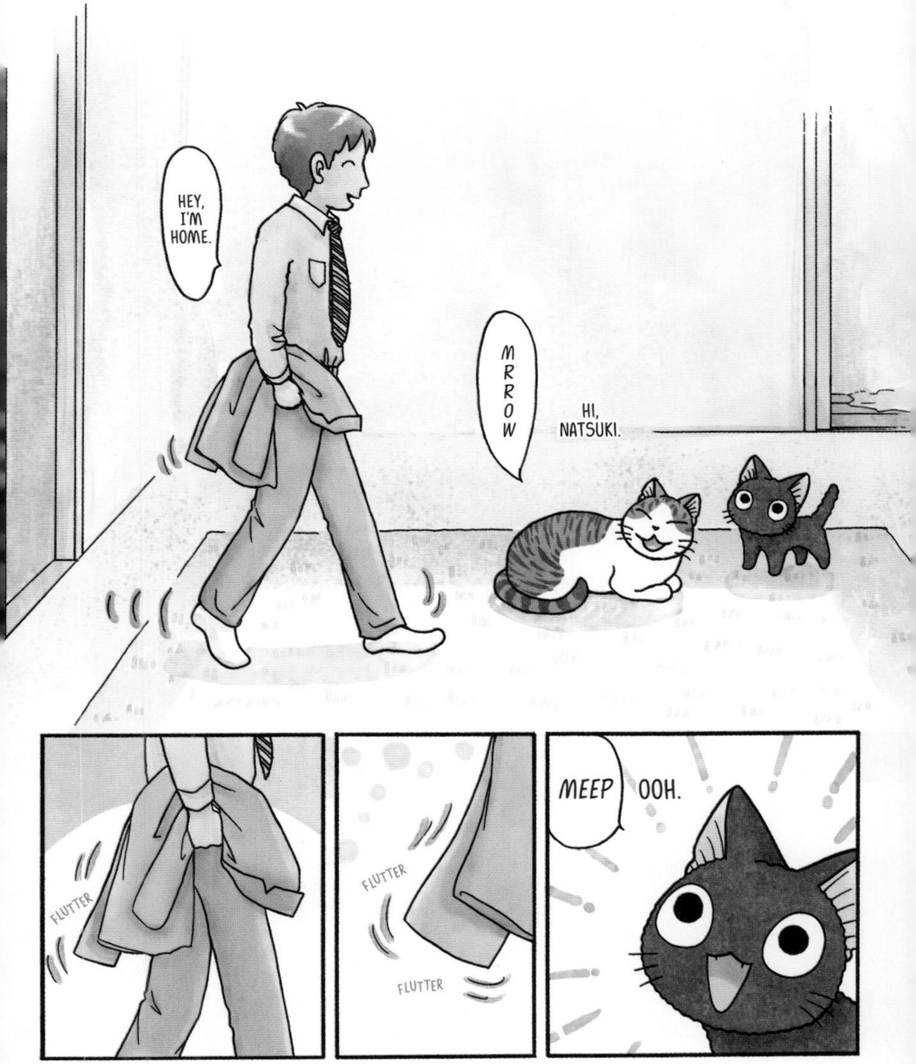
HEY, I'M HOME.
MRROW
HI, NATSUKI.
FLUTTER
FLUTTER
FLUTTER
MEEP
OOH.

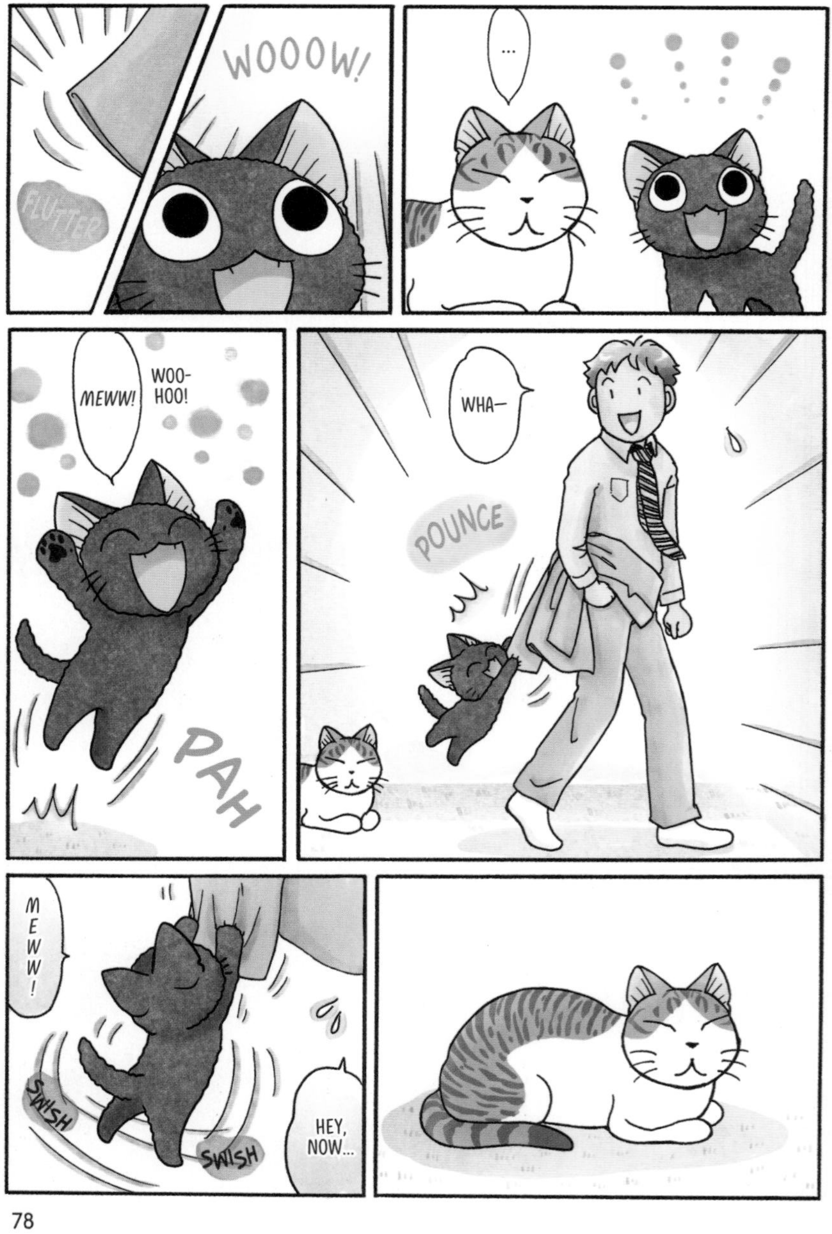
FLUTTER
WOOOW!
...
MEWW!
WOO-HOO!
PAH
WHA—
POUNCE
MEWW!
SWISH
SWISH
HEY, NOW...

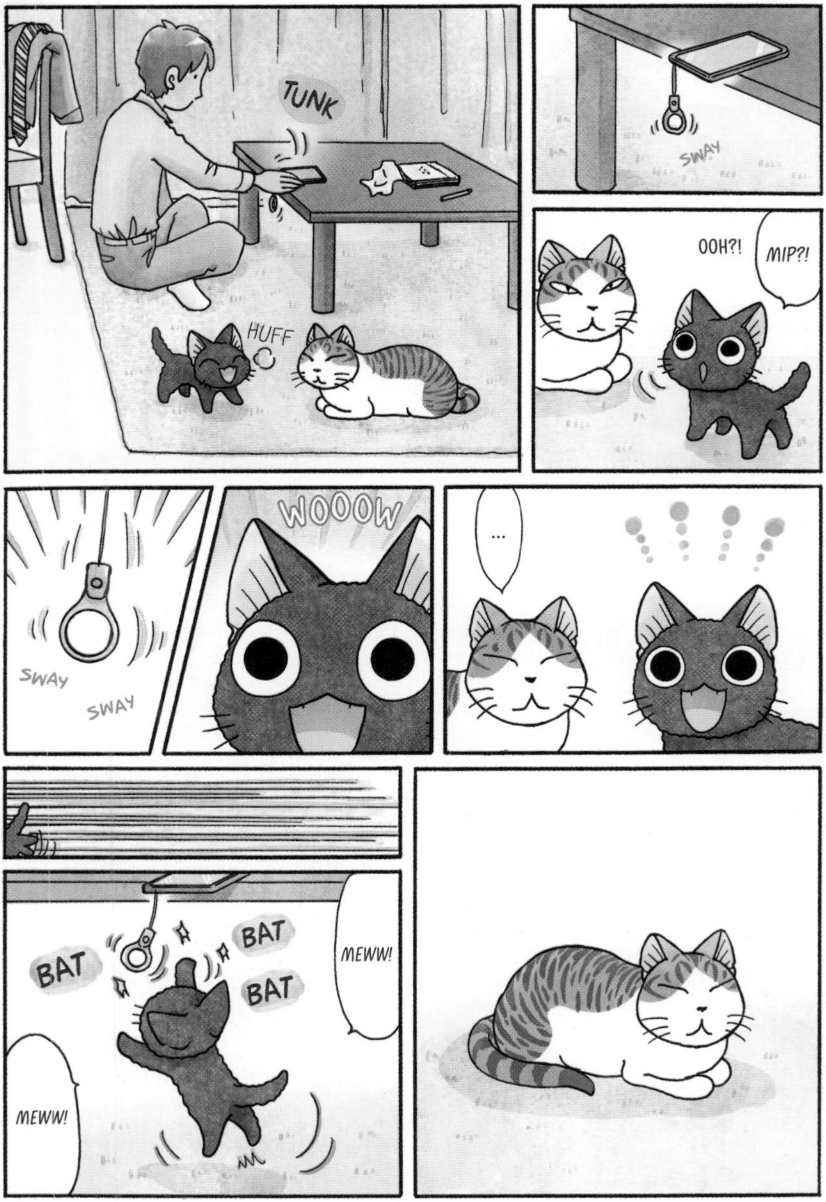
TUNK
HUFF
SWAY
OOH?!
MIP?!
SWAY
SWAY
WOOOW
...
BAT
BAT
BAT
MEWW!
MEWW!

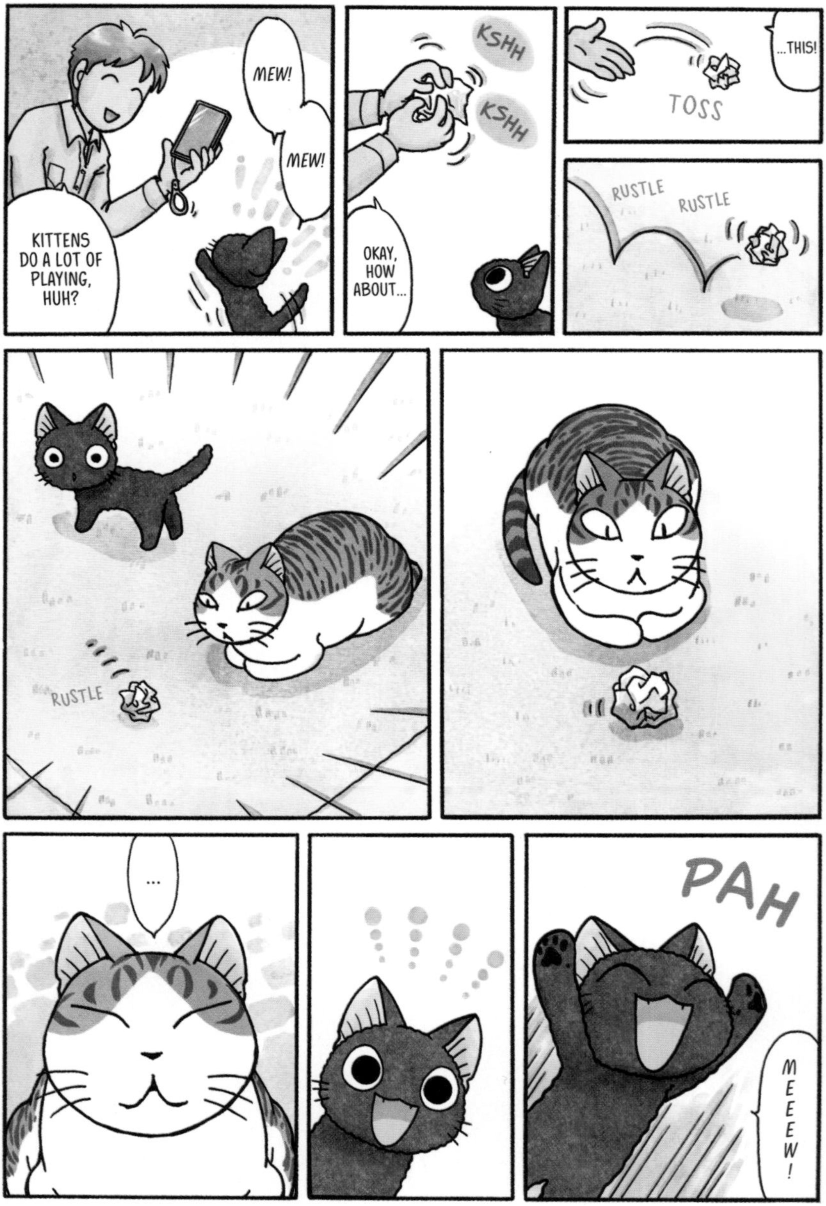
MEW!
MEW!
KITTENS DO A LOT OF PLAYING, HUH?
KSHH
KSHH
OKAY, HOW ABOUT...
TOSS
...THIS!
RUSTLE
RUSTLE
RUSTLE
...
PAH
MEEEW!

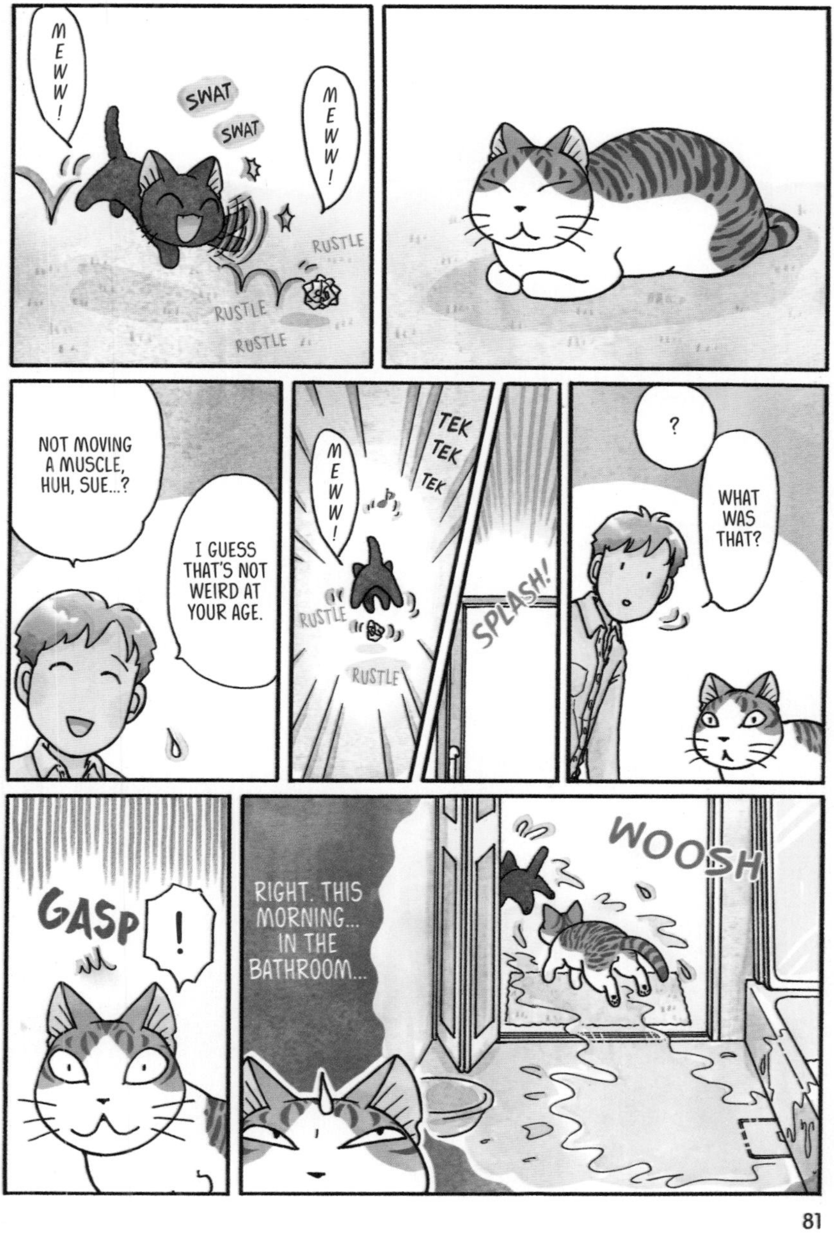
MEWW!
SWAT
SWAT
MEWW!
RUSTLE
RUSTLE
RUSTLE
NOT MOVING A MUSCLE, HUH, SUE...?
I GUESS THAT'S NOT WEIRD AT YOUR AGE.
MEWW!
TEK
TEK
TEK
RUSTLE
RUSTLE
SPLASH!
?
WHAT WAS THAT?
GASP
!
RIGHT. THIS MORNING... IN THE BATHROOM...
WOOSH

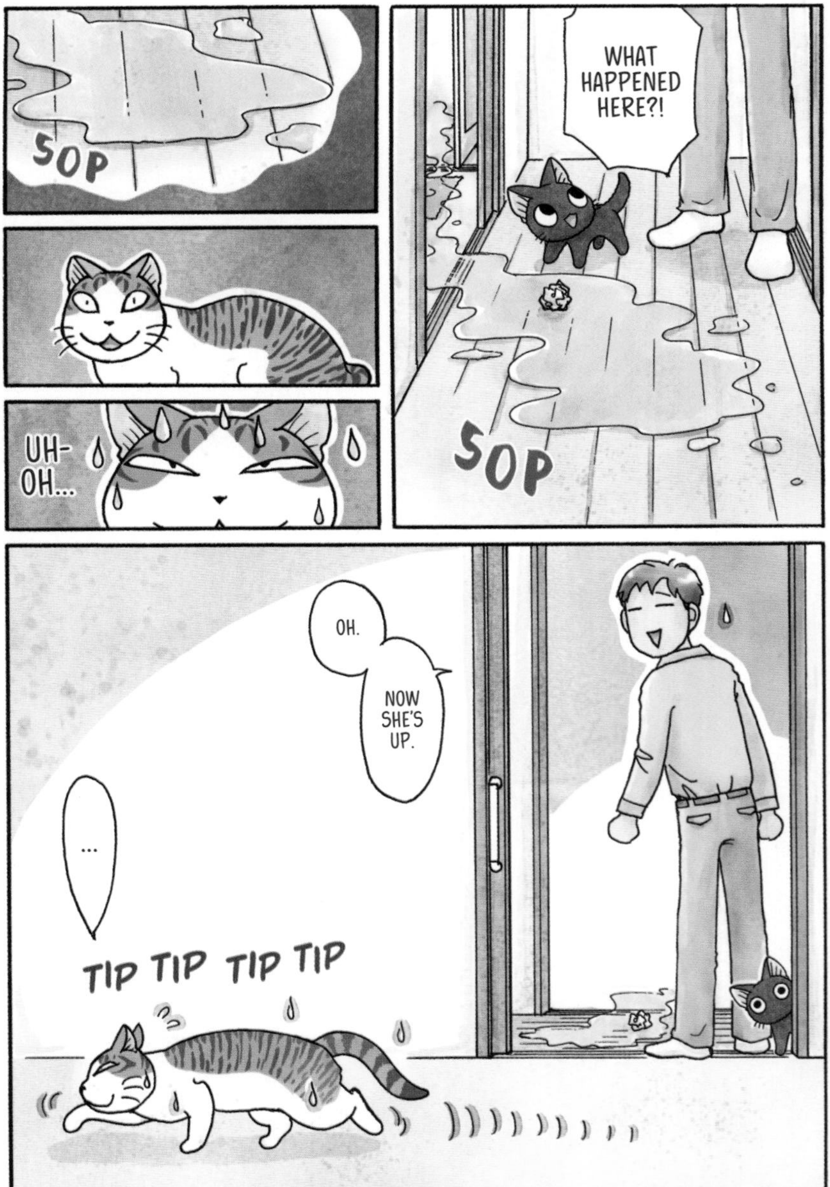
SOP
UH-OH...
WHAT HAPPENED HERE?!
SOP
OH.
NOW SHE'S UP.
...
TIP TIP TIP TIP

Sue & Tai-chan

CHAPTER 12 Sue Loses Her Cool

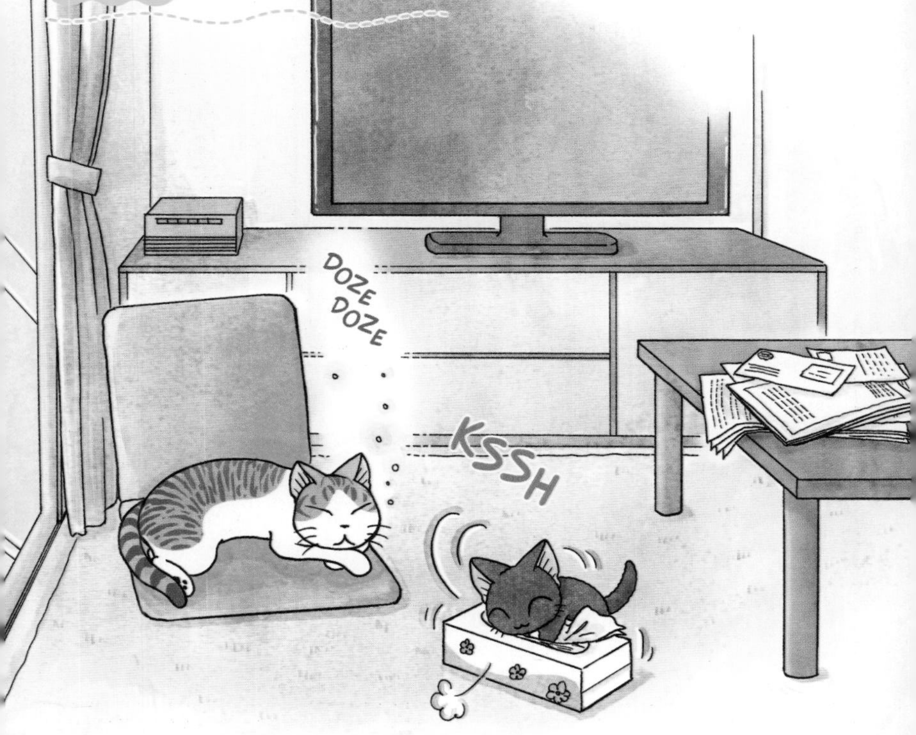
DOZE
DOZE
KSSH

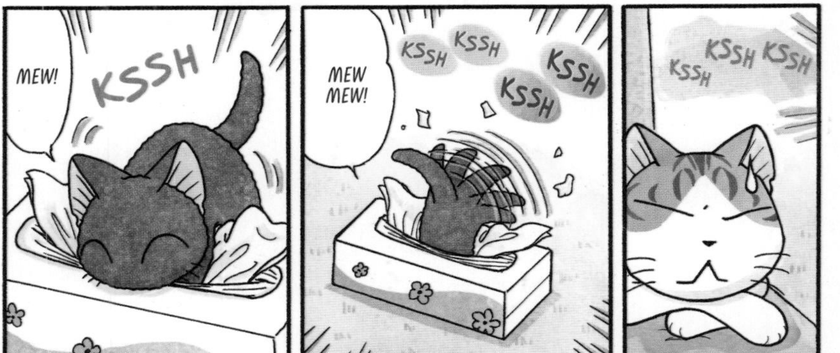
MEW!
KSSH
MEW MEW!
KSSH
KSSH
KSSH
KSSH
KSSH
KSSH
KSSH

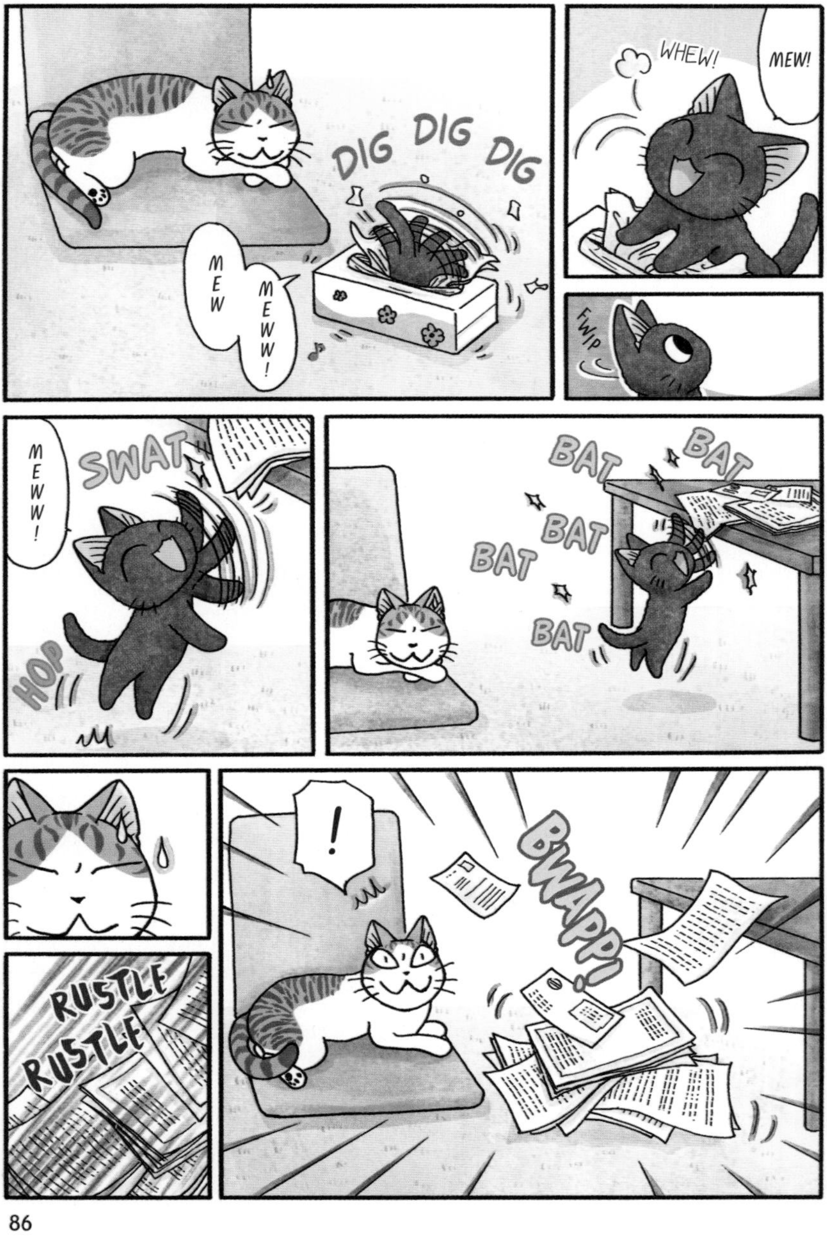
DIG DIG DIG
MEW MEWW!
WHEW!
MEW!
FWIP
MEWW!
SWAT
HOP
BAT BAT BAT BAT BAT
RUSTLE RUSTLE
!
BWAPP!

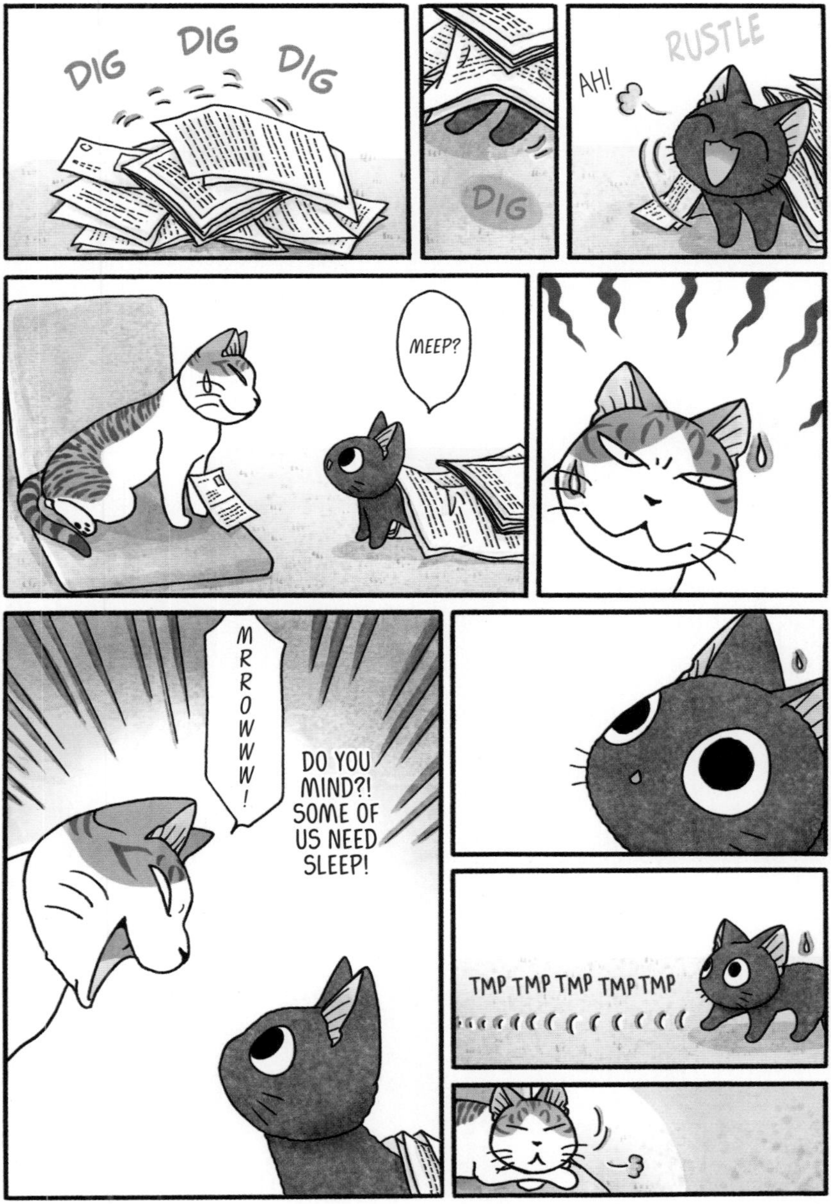
DIG DIG DIG
DIG
AH!
RUSTLE
MEEP?
MRROWWW!
DO YOU MIND?! SOME OF US NEED SLEEP!
TMP TMP TMP TMP TMP

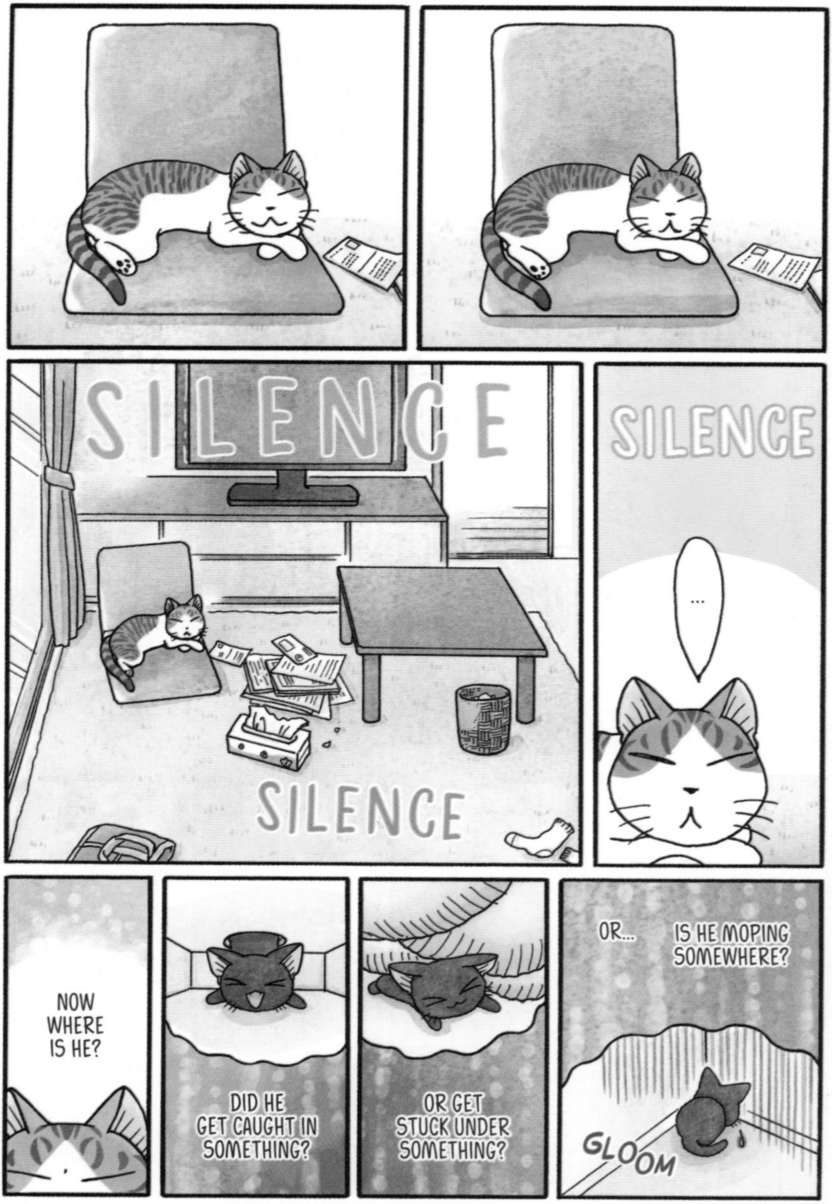
SILENCE
SILENCE
SILENCE
...
NOW WHERE IS HE?
DID HE GET CAUGHT IN SOMETHING?
OR GET STUCK UNDER SOMETHING?
OR...
IS HE MOPING SOMEWHERE?
GLOOM

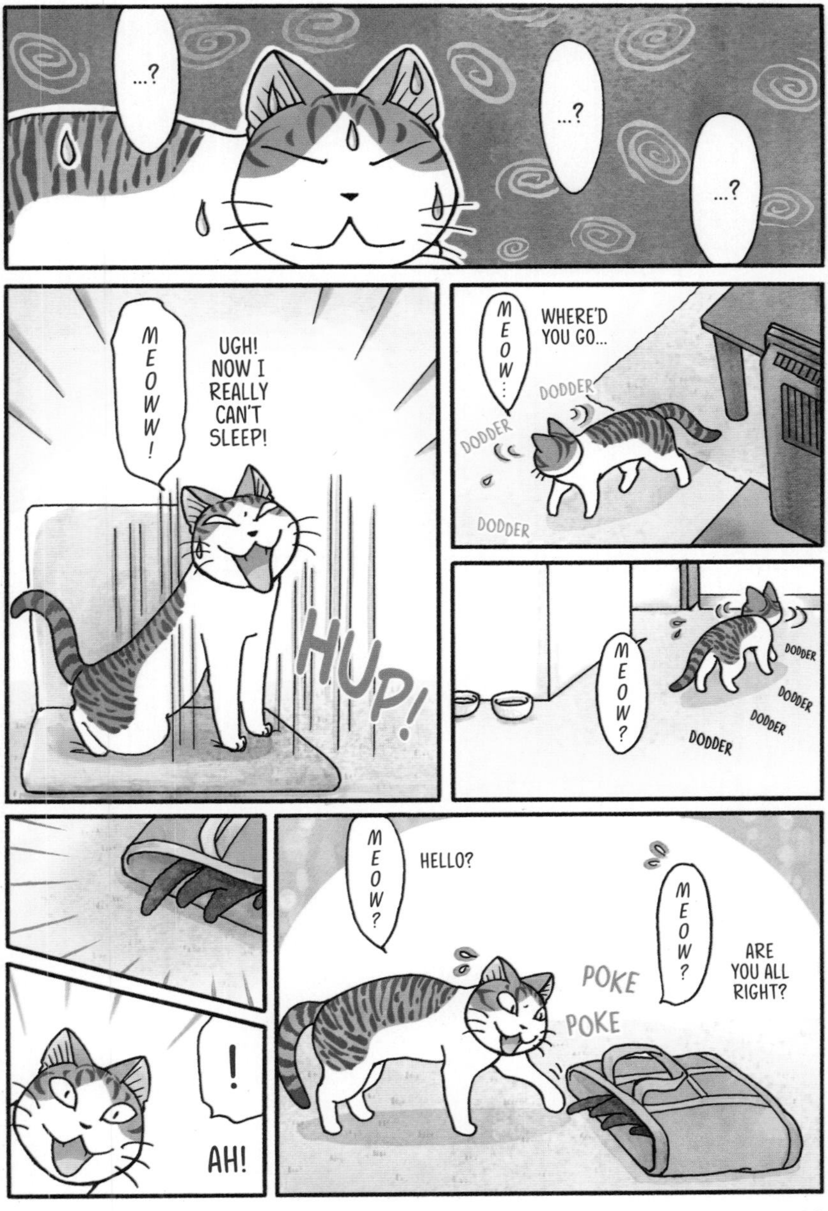
...?
...?
...?
MEOWW!
UGH! NOW I REALLY CAN'T SLEEP!
HUP!
MEOW...
WHERE'D YOU GO...
DODDER
DODDER
DODDER
MEOW?
DODDER
DODDER
DODDER
DODDER
!
AH!
MEOW?
HELLO?
POKE
POKE
MEOW?
ARE YOU ALL RIGHT?

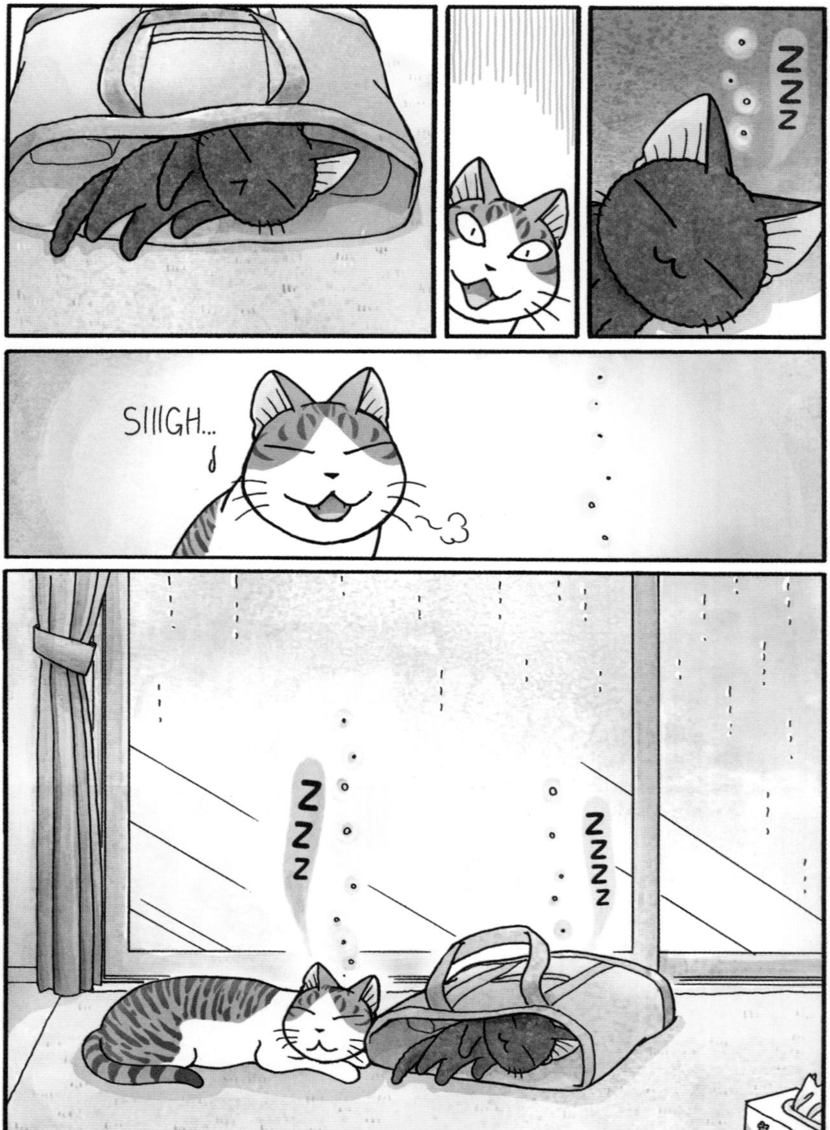
ZZZ
SIIIGH...
ZZZ
ZZZZ

CHAPTER 13 Open Up, Door!

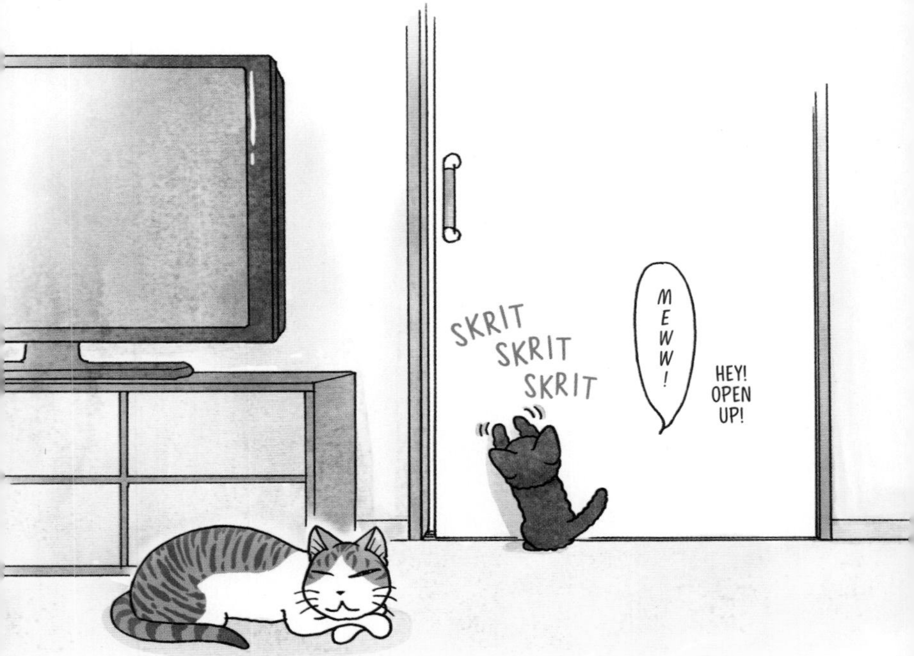
SKRIT
SKRIT
SKRIT
MEWW!
HEY! OPEN UP!

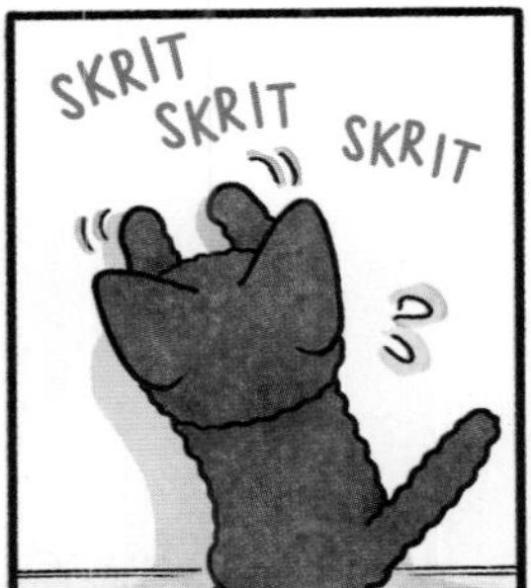
SKRIT
SKRIT
SKRIT

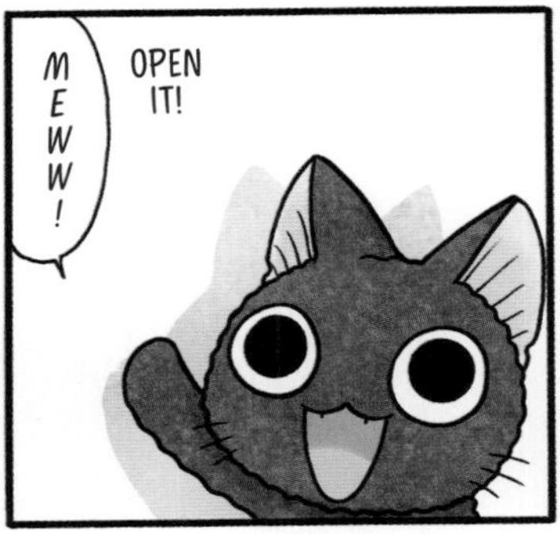
MEWW!
OPEN IT!

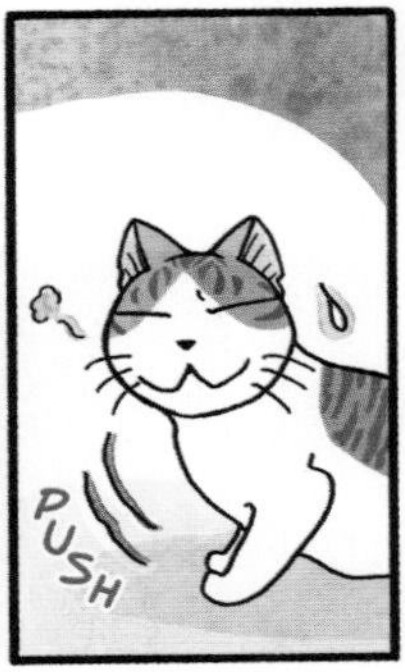
PUSH

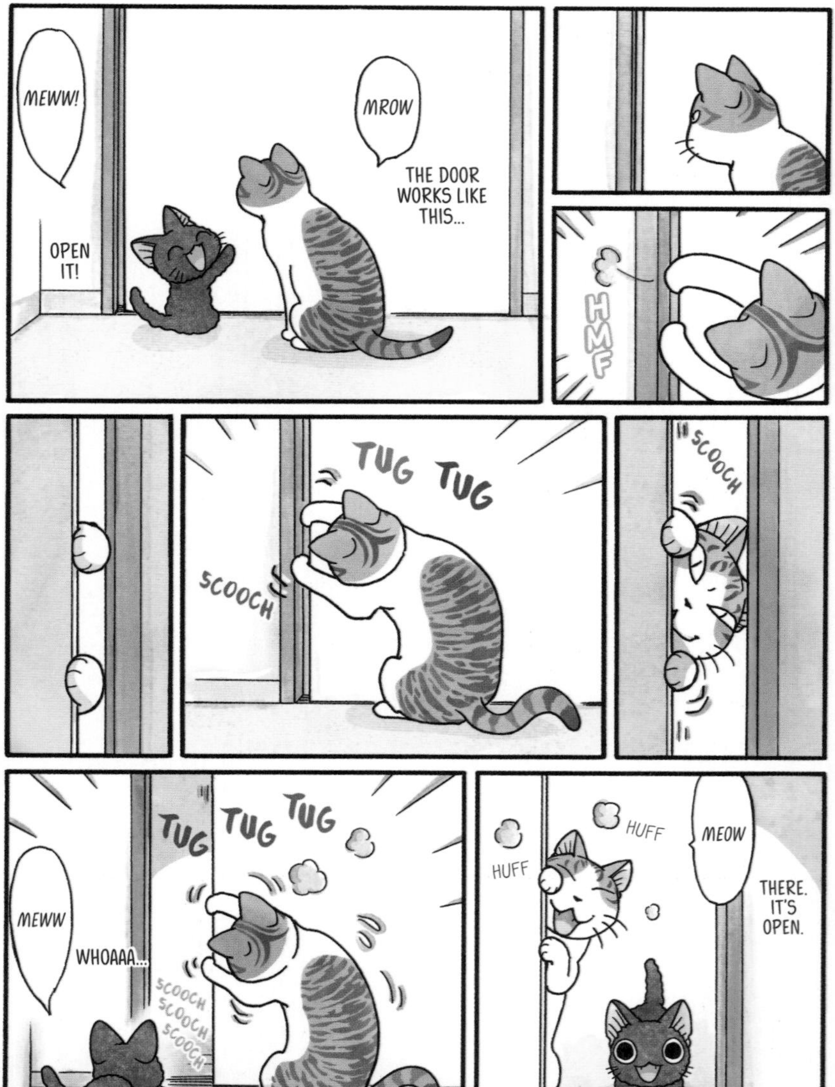
MEWW!
OPEN IT!
MROW
THE DOOR WORKS LIKE THIS...
HMF
TUG TUG
SCOOCH
SCOOCH
TUG TUG TUG
MEWW
WHOAAA...
SCOOCH SCOOCH SCOOCH
HUFF
HUFF
MEOW
THERE. IT'S OPEN.

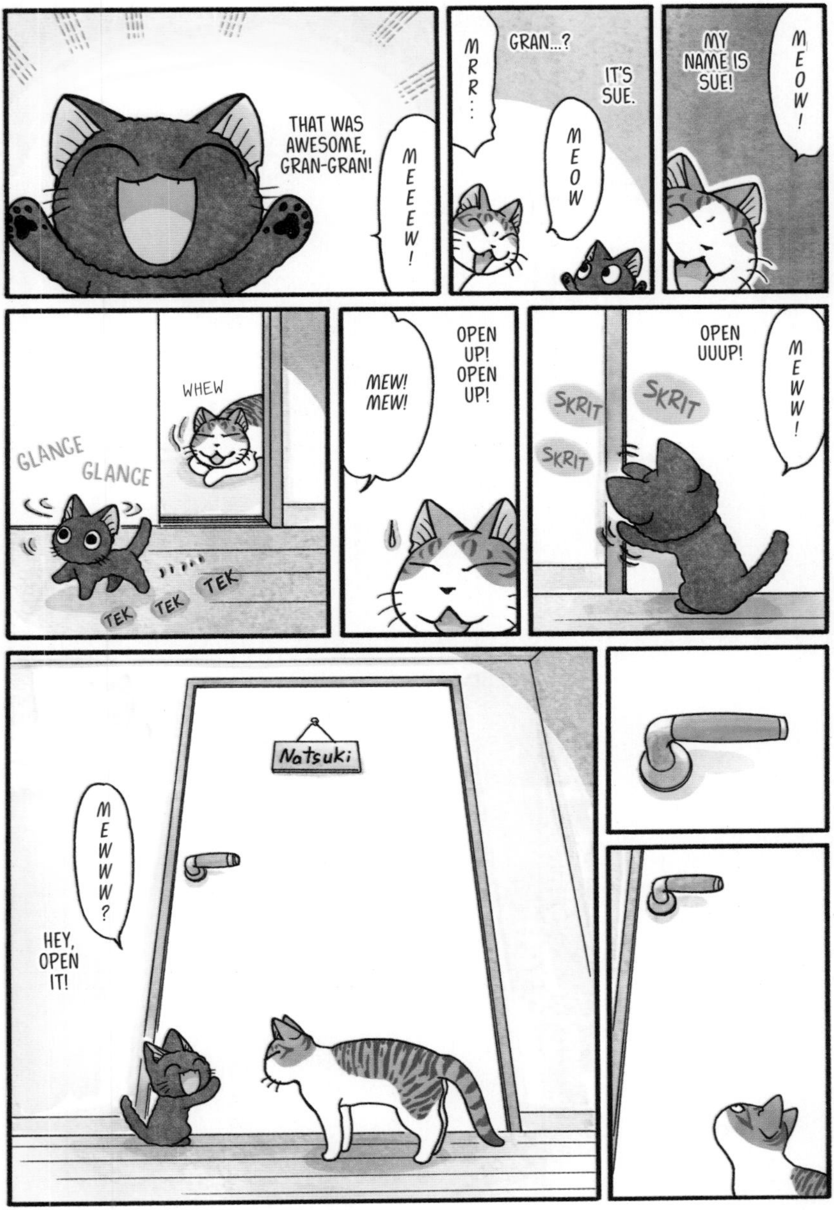
THAT WAS AWESOME, GRAN-GRAN!
MEEEEW!
MRR...
GRAN...?
IT'S SUE.
MEOW
MY NAME IS SUE!
MEOW!
WHEW
GLANCE
GLANCE
TEK
TEK
TEK
MEW! MEW!
OPEN UP! OPEN UP!
SKRIT
SKRIT
SKRIT
OPEN UUUP!
MEWW!
Natsuki
MEWWW?
HEY, OPEN IT!

HNG
NNNGH
MROWW...
CAN'T... REACH...
HNNNG
TREMBLE...
MROW!
UPSY!
SHMP
SHMP
HUFF
MROW—
UPSY—
HUFF
MROW!
—DAISY!
BOING
SHMP
BOING
SHMP
HUFF
HUFF
TAK!

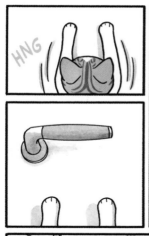

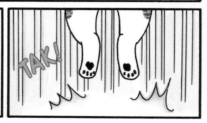

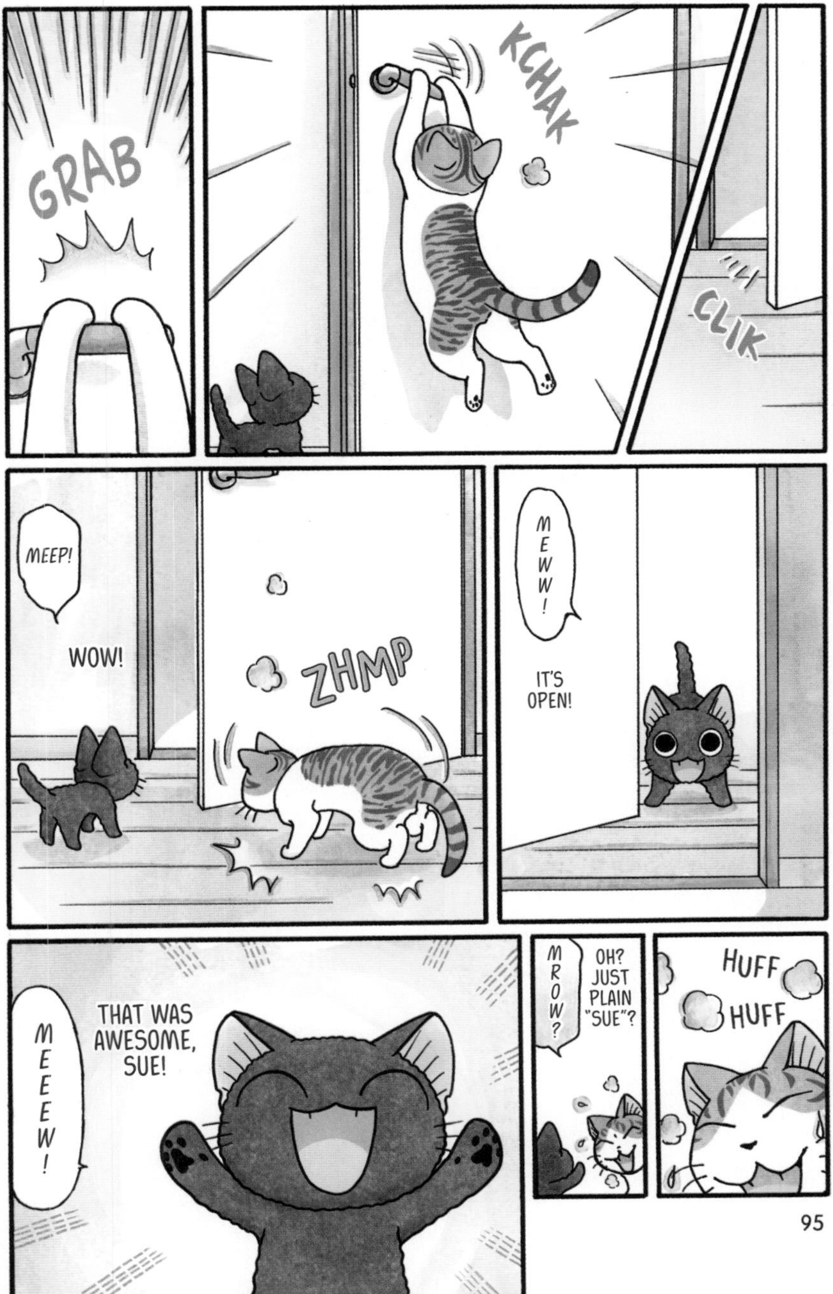
GRAB
KCHAK
CLIK
MEEP!
WOW!
ZHMP
MEWW!
IT'S OPEN!
MEEEW!
THAT WAS AWESOME, SUE!
MROW?
OH? JUST PLAIN "SUE"?
HUFF HUFF

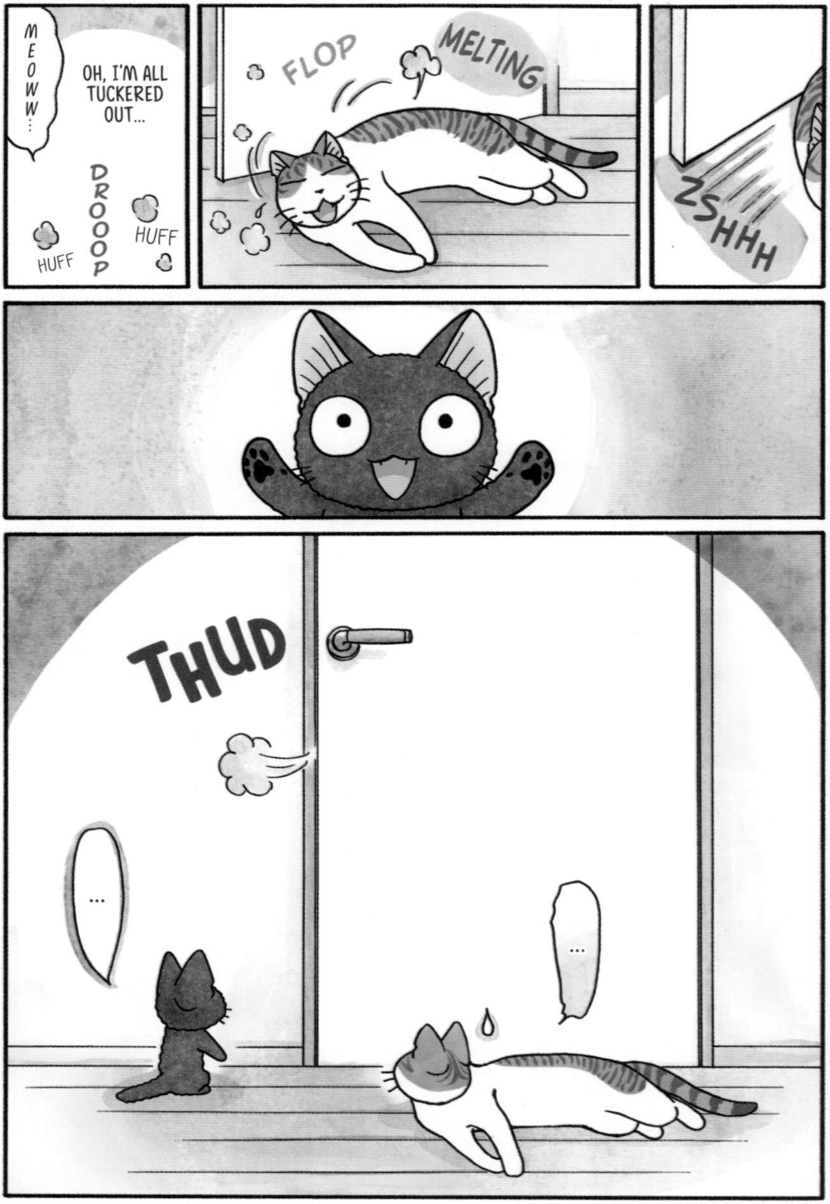
MEOWW…
OH, I'M ALL TUCKERED OUT...
DROOOP
HUFF
HUFF
FLOP
MELTING
ZSHHH
THUD
...
...

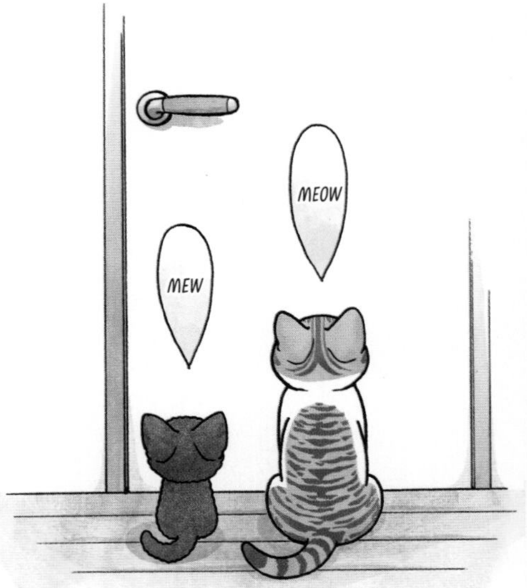
MEOW
MEW

Sue & Tai-chan

CHAPTER 14 Watermelon Encounter

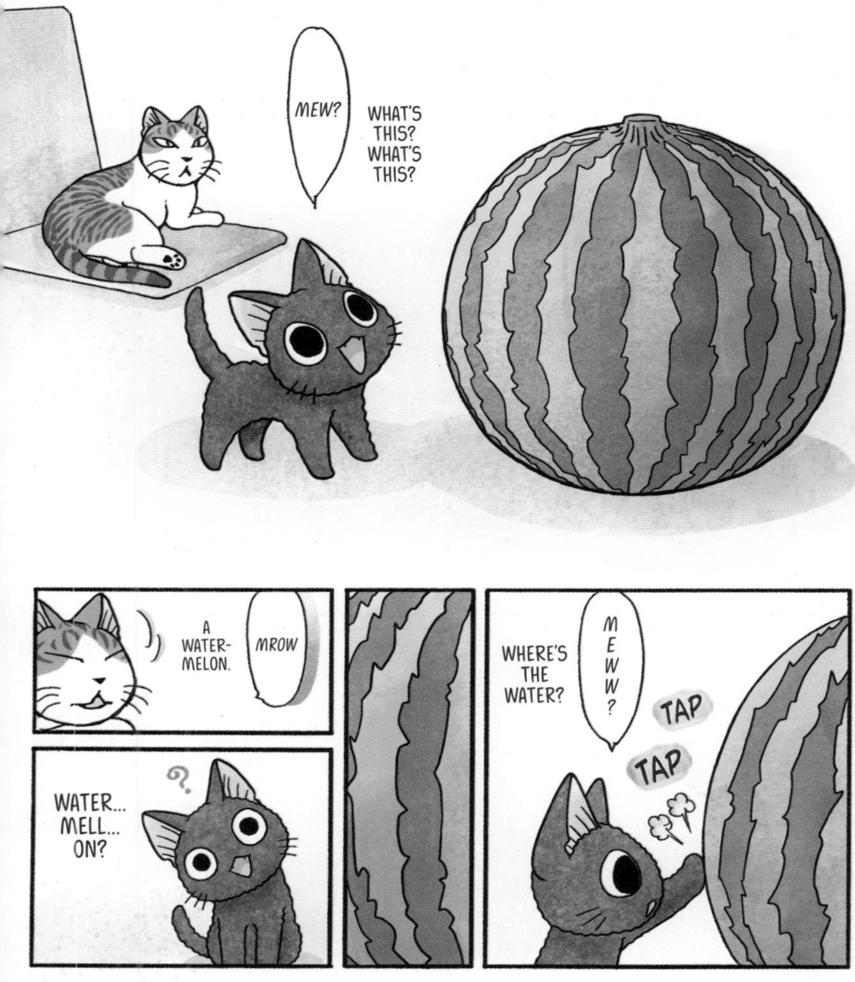
MEW?
WHAT'S THIS? WHAT'S THIS?
A WATER-MELON.
MROW
WATER... MELL... ON?
WHERE'S THE WATER?
MEWW?
TAP
TAP

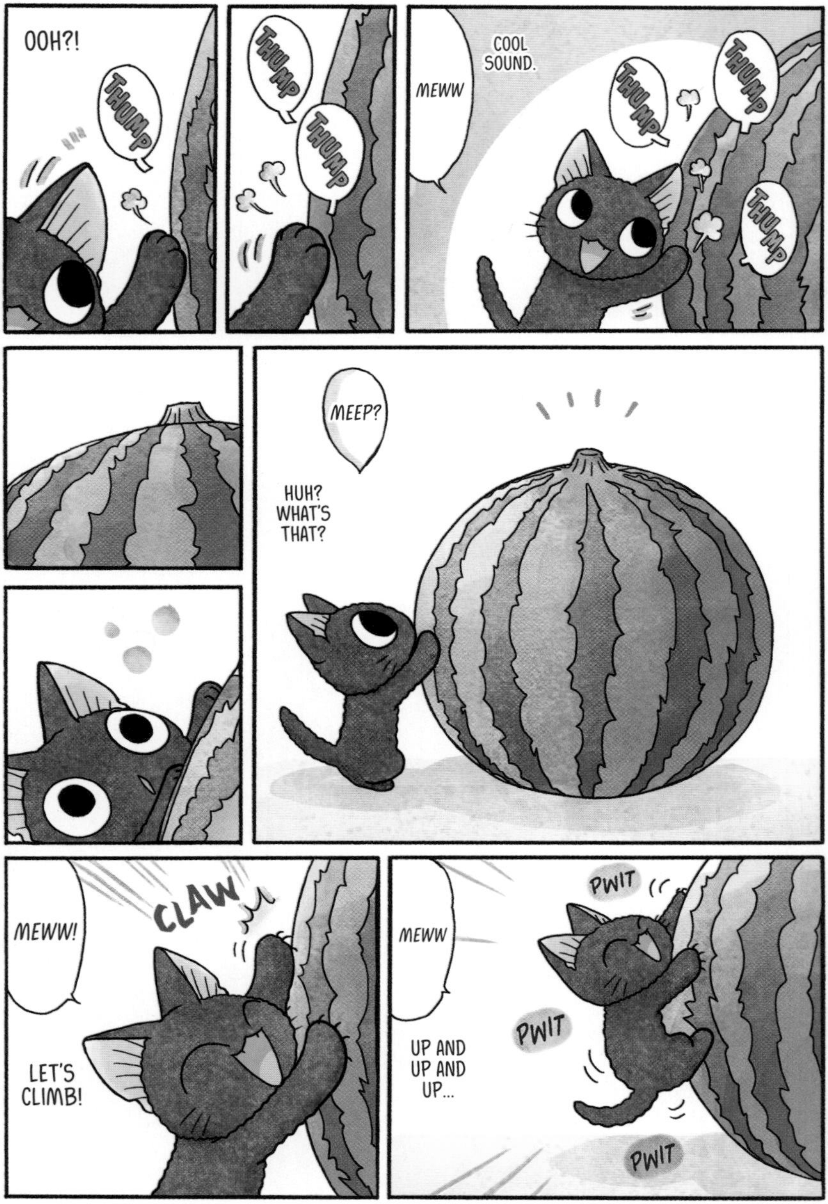
OOH?!
THUMP
THUMP
THUMP
MEWW
COOL SOUND.
THUMP
THUMP
THUMP
MEEP?
HUH? WHAT'S THAT?
MEWW!
CLAW
LET'S CLIMB!
MEWW
PWIT
PWIT
UP AND UP AND UP...
PWIT

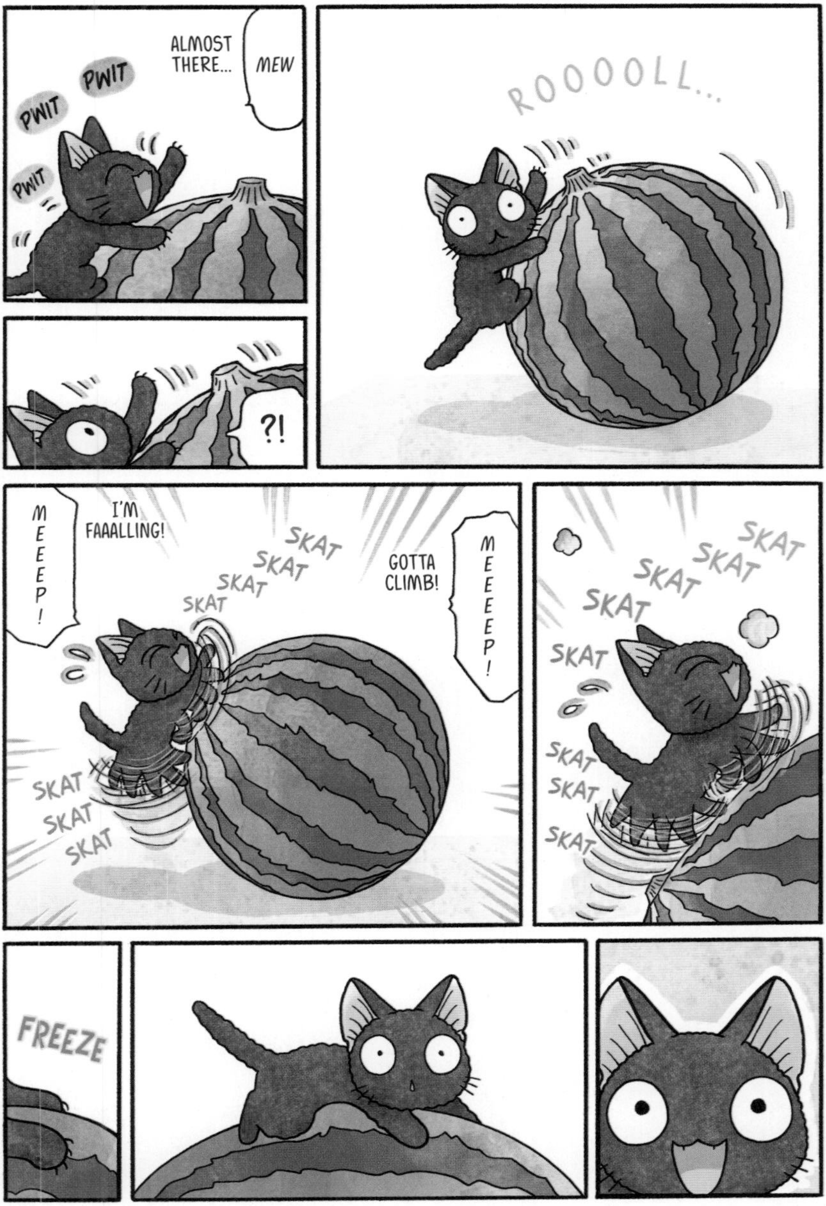
PWIT
PWIT
PWIT
ALMOST THERE...
MEW
?!
ROOOOLL...
MEEEP!
I'M FAAALLING!
SKAT
SKAT
SKAT
SKAT
GOTTA CLIMB!
MEEEEP!
SKAT
SKAT
SKAT
SKAT
SKAT
SKAT
SKAT
SKAT
SKAT
SKAT
SKAT
FREEZE

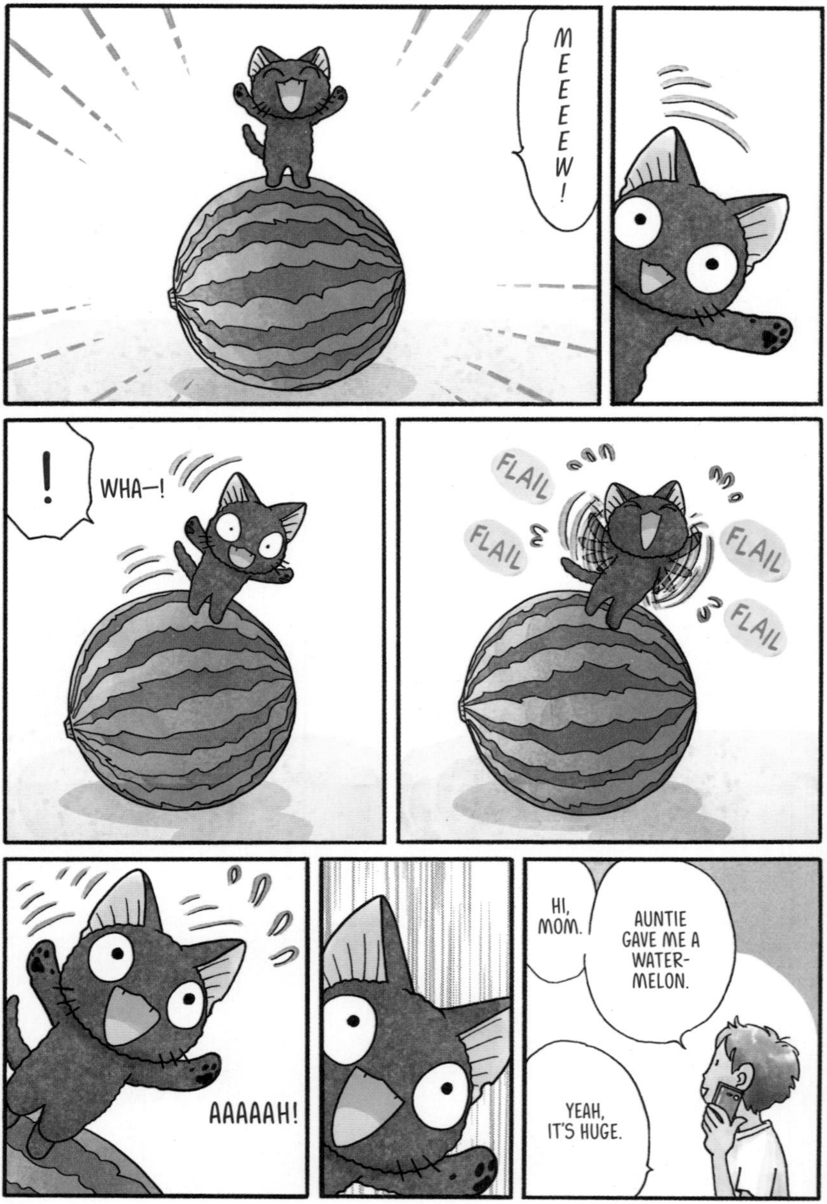
MEEEEEW!
!
WHA—!
FLAIL
FLAIL
FLAIL
FLAIL
AAAAAH!
HI, MOM.
AUNTIE GAVE ME A WATER-MELON.
YEAH, IT'S HUGE.

I DON'T KNOW HOW I'LL GET IT IN THE FRIDGE.

MEWWWW!

MEEEEEP!

SKAT SKAT SKAT SKAT SKAT SKAT

ROLL ROLL

MEEEEEP!

SKAT SKAT SKAT

SKAT SKAT SKAT

ROLL ROLL

MEEP!

ABANDON SHIP!

TAK

ROLL ROLL

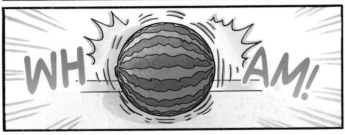

WH—AM!

CRACK

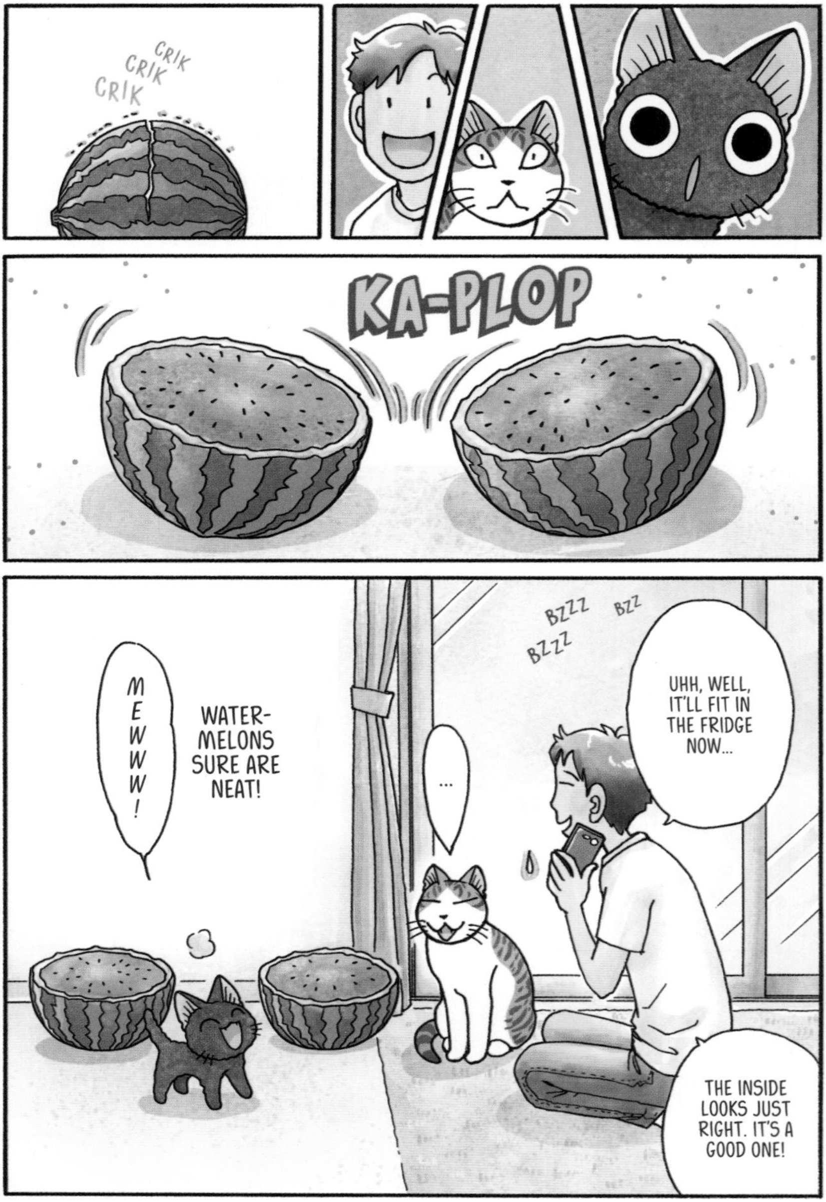
CRIK
CRIK
CRIK
KA-PLOP
MEWWWW!
WATER-MELONS SURE ARE NEAT!
...
BZZZ
BZZZ
BZZ
UHH, WELL, IT'LL FIT IN THE FRIDGE NOW...
THE INSIDE LOOKS JUST RIGHT. IT'S A GOOD ONE!

CHAPTER 15 Debut of an Amazing Ball!

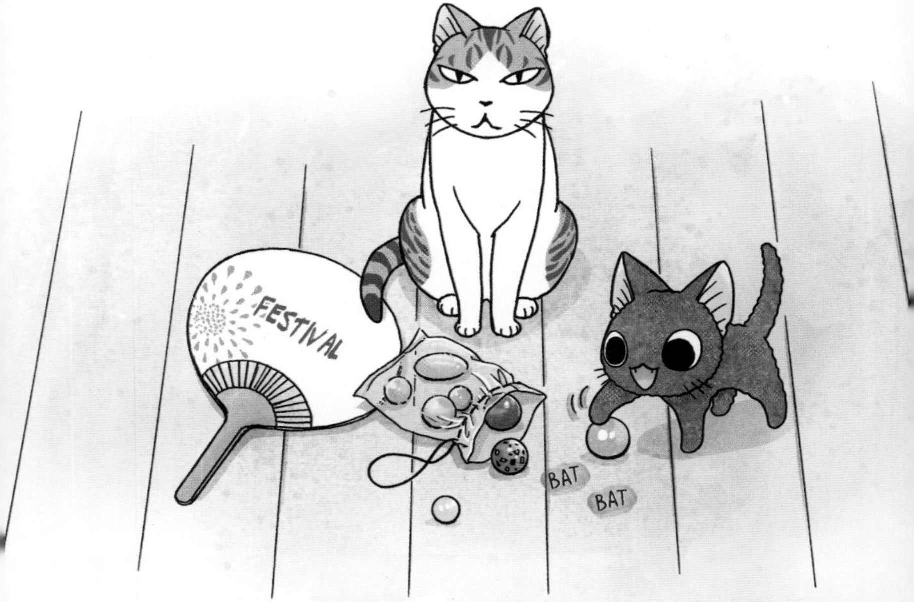
FESTIVAL
BAT
BAT

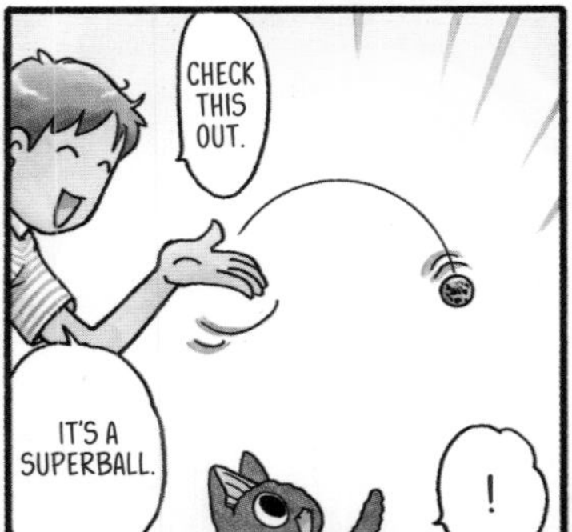
CHECK THIS OUT.
IT'S A SUPERBALL.
!

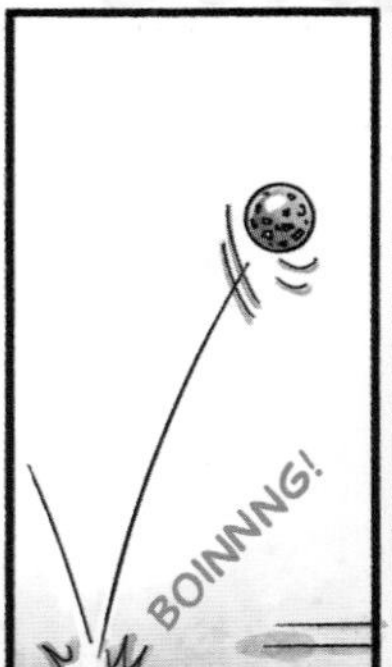
BOINNNG!

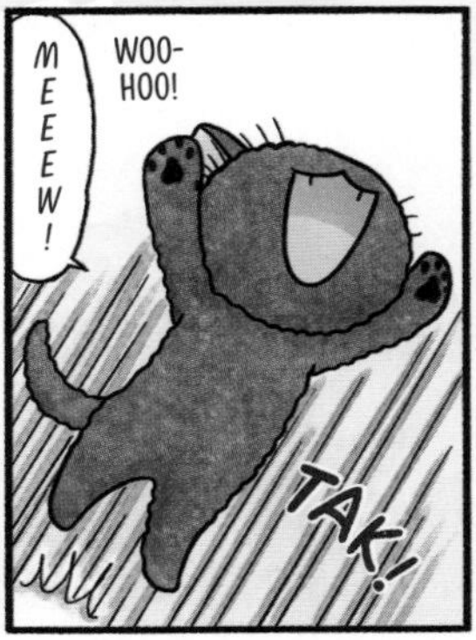
MEEEEW!
WOO-HOO!
TAK!

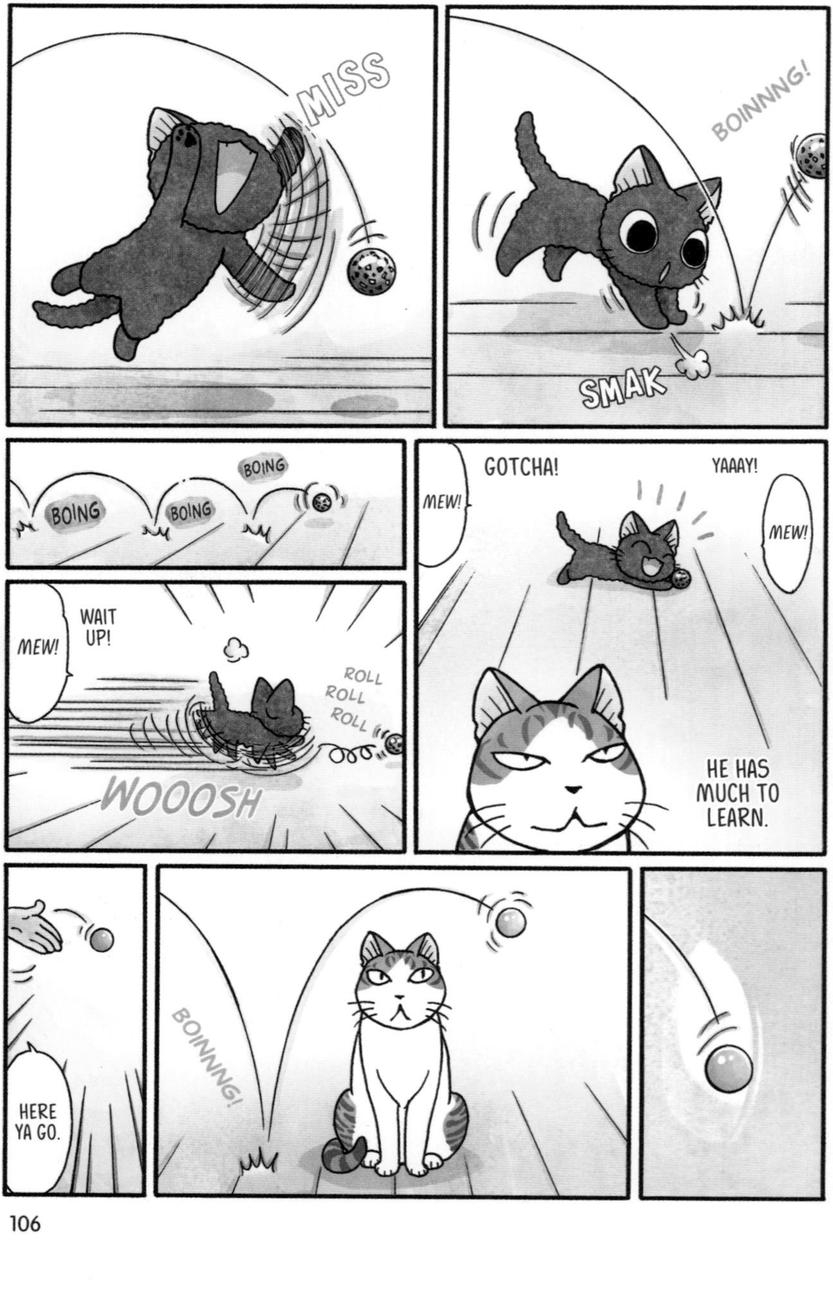
MISS
BOINNNG!
SMAK
BOING
BOING
BOING
MEW!
WAIT UP!
ROLL
ROLL
ROLL
WOOOSH
MEW!
GOTCHA!
YAAAY!
MEW!
HE HAS MUCH TO LEARN.
HERE YA GO.
BOINNNG!

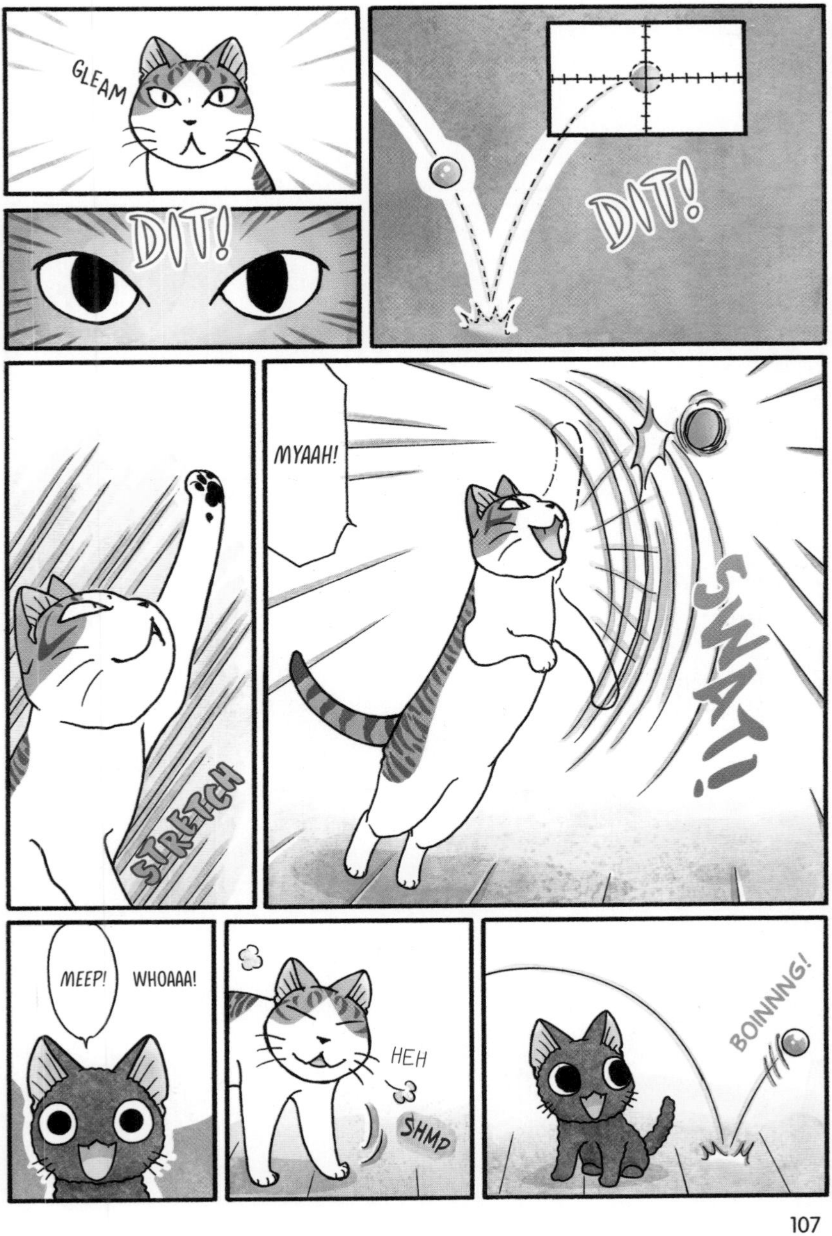
GLEAM
DIT!
DIT!
MYAAH!
STRETCH
SWAT!!
MEEP!
WHOAAA!
HEH
SHMP
BOINNNG!

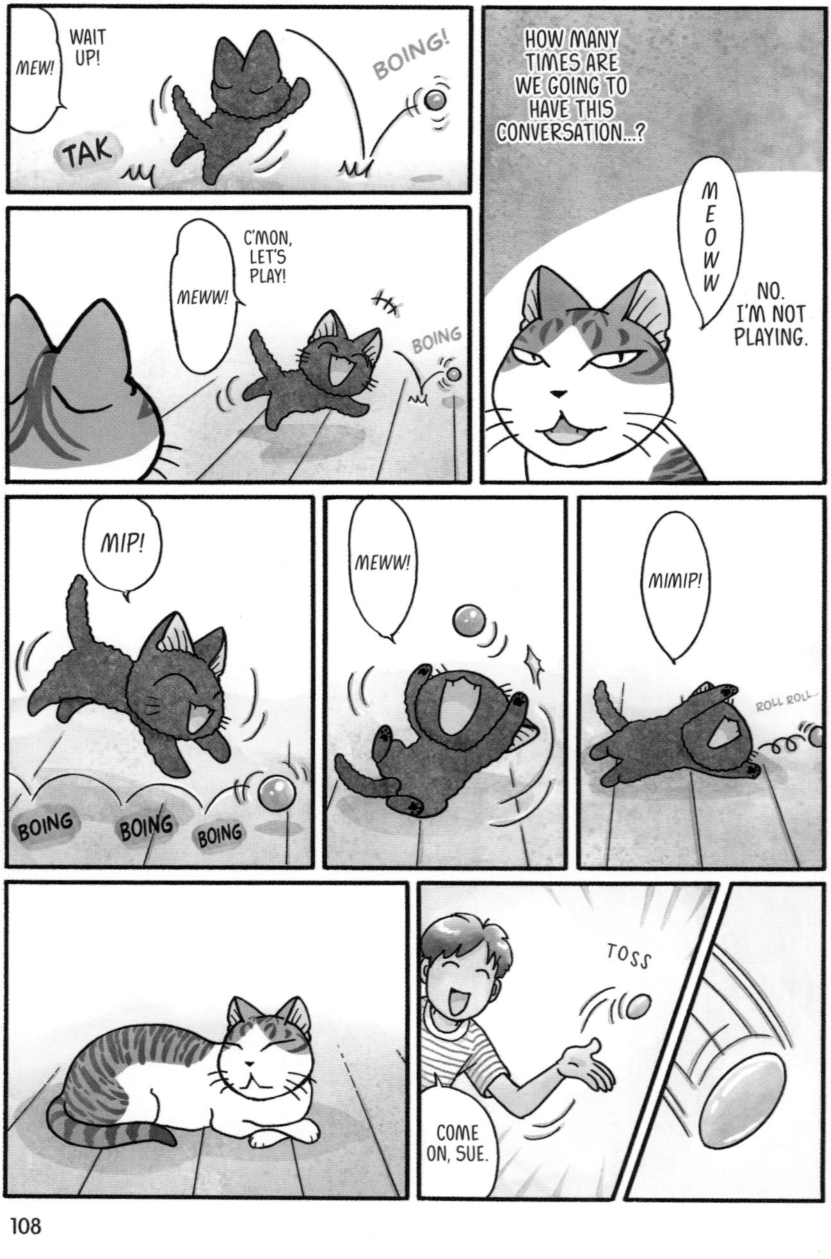
MEW!
WAIT UP!
BOING!
TAK
MEWW!
C'MON, LET'S PLAY!
BOING
HOW MANY TIMES ARE WE GOING TO HAVE THIS CONVERSATION...?
MEOWW
NO. I'M NOT PLAYING.
MIP!
BOING
BOING
BOING
MEWW!
MIMIP!
ROLL ROLL...
TOSS
COME ON, SUE.

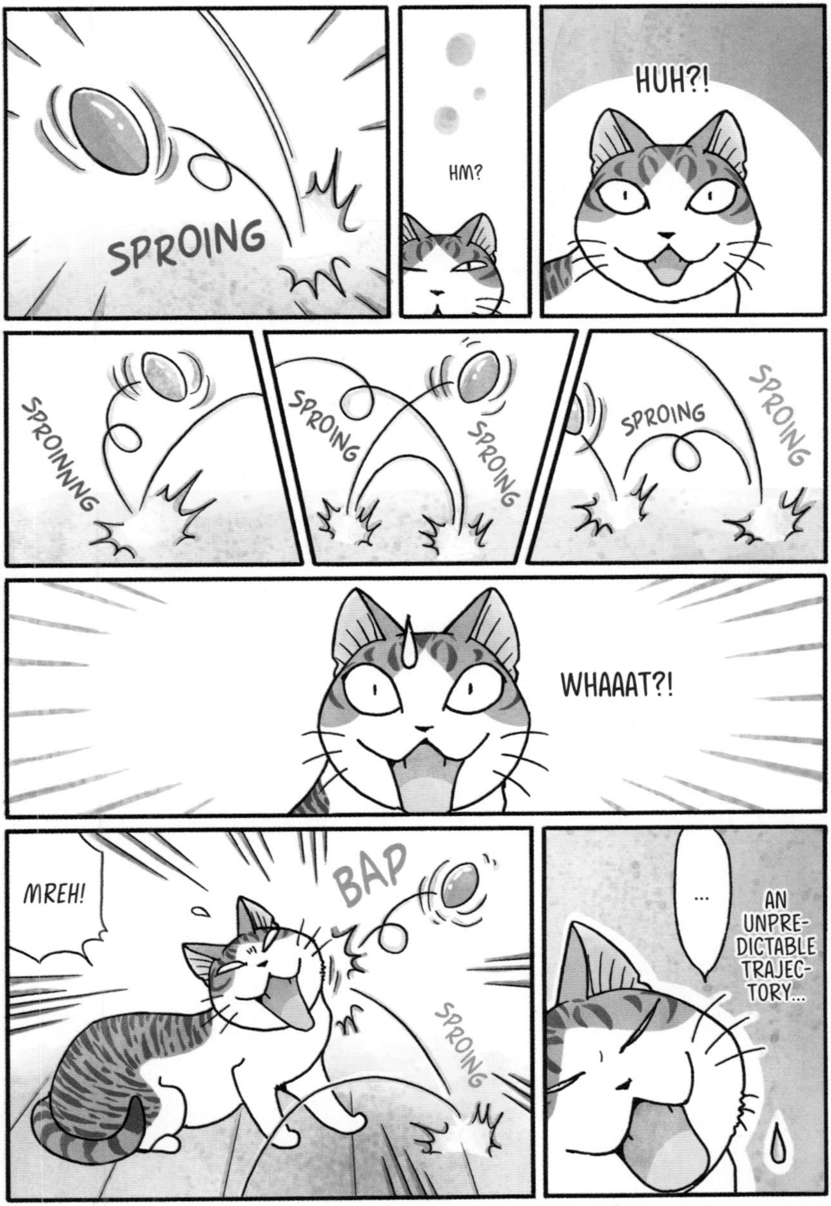
SPROING
HM?
HUH?!
SPROINNNG
SPROING
SPROING
SPROING
SPROING
WHAAAT?!
MREH!
BAP
SPROING
...
AN UNPRE-DICTABLE TRAJEC-TORY...

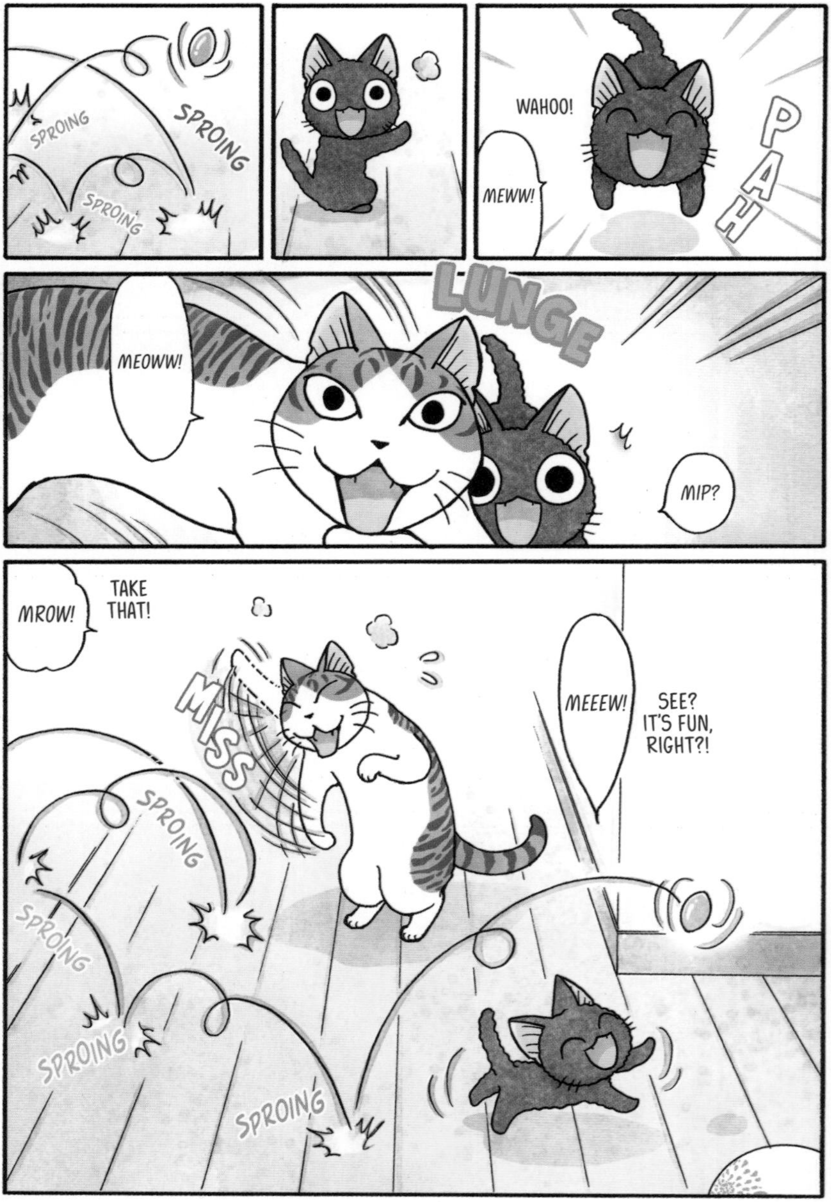
SPROING
SPROING
SPROING
WAHOO!
MEWW!
PAH
MEOWW!
LUNGE
MIP?
MROW!
TAKE THAT!
MISS
MEEEW!
SEE? IT'S FUN, RIGHT?!
SPROING
SPROING
SPROING
SPROING

CHAPTER 16 Let's Play Hide-and-Seek!

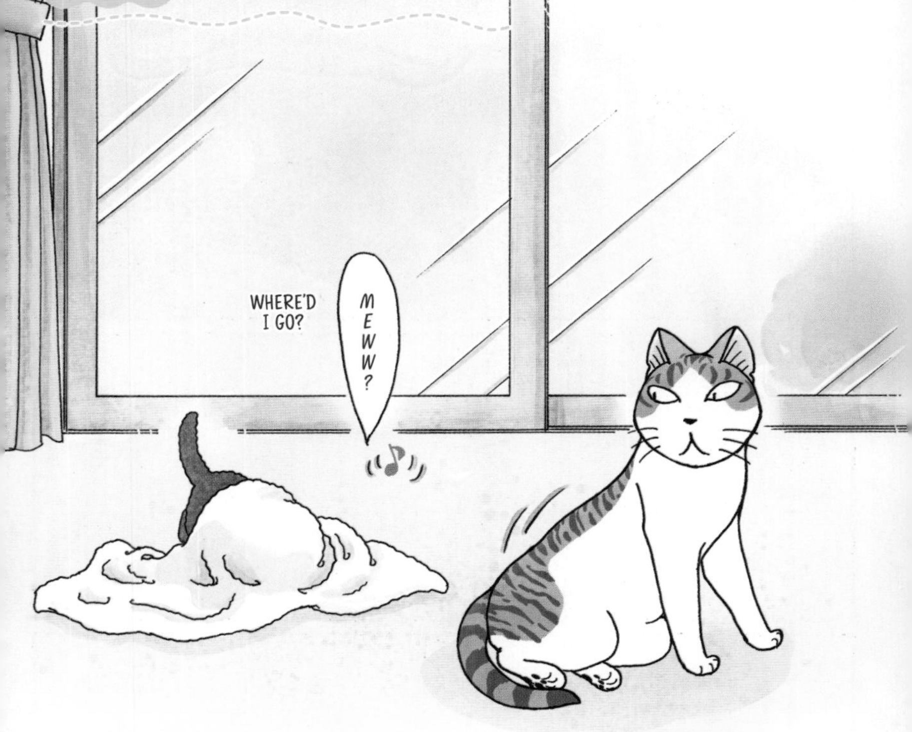
WHERE'D I GO?
MEWW?

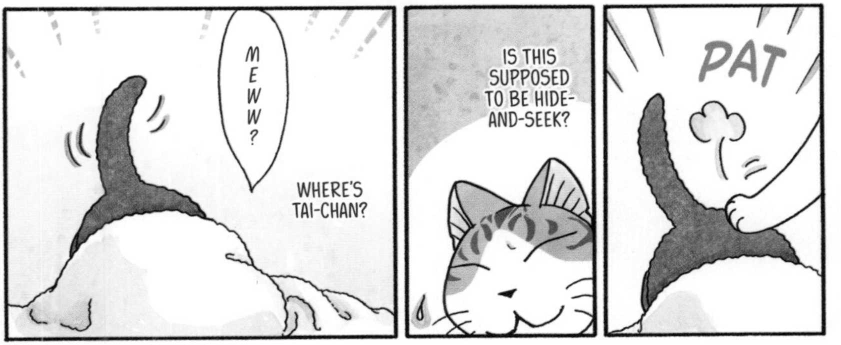
MEWW?
WHERE'S TAI-CHAN?
IS THIS SUPPOSED TO BE HIDE-AND-SEEK?
PAT

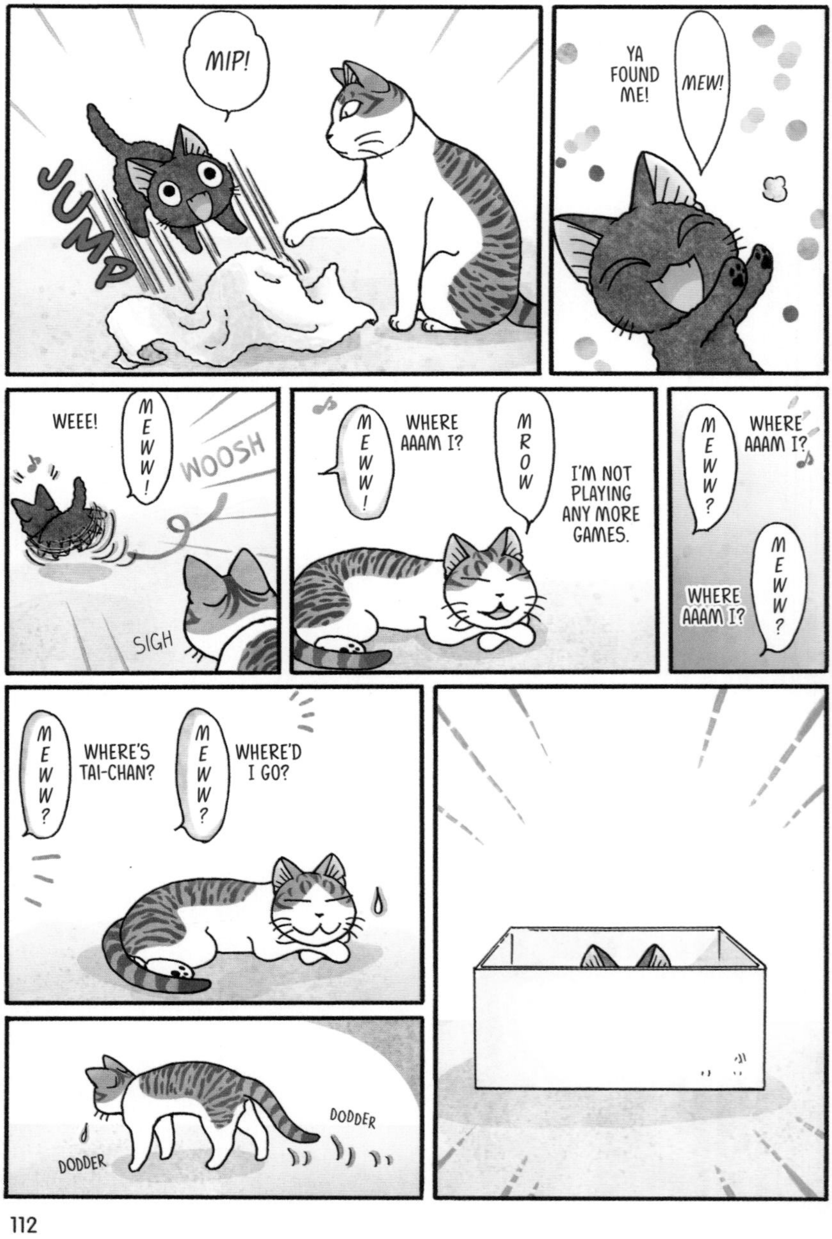
MIP!
JUMP
YA FOUND ME!
MEW!
WEEE!
MEWW!
WOOSH
SIGH
MEWW!
WHERE AAAM I?
MROW
I'M NOT PLAYING ANY MORE GAMES.
MEWW?
WHERE AAAM I?
MEWW?
WHERE AAAM I?
MEWW?
WHERE'S TAI-CHAN?
MEWW?
WHERE'D I GO?
DODDER
DODDER

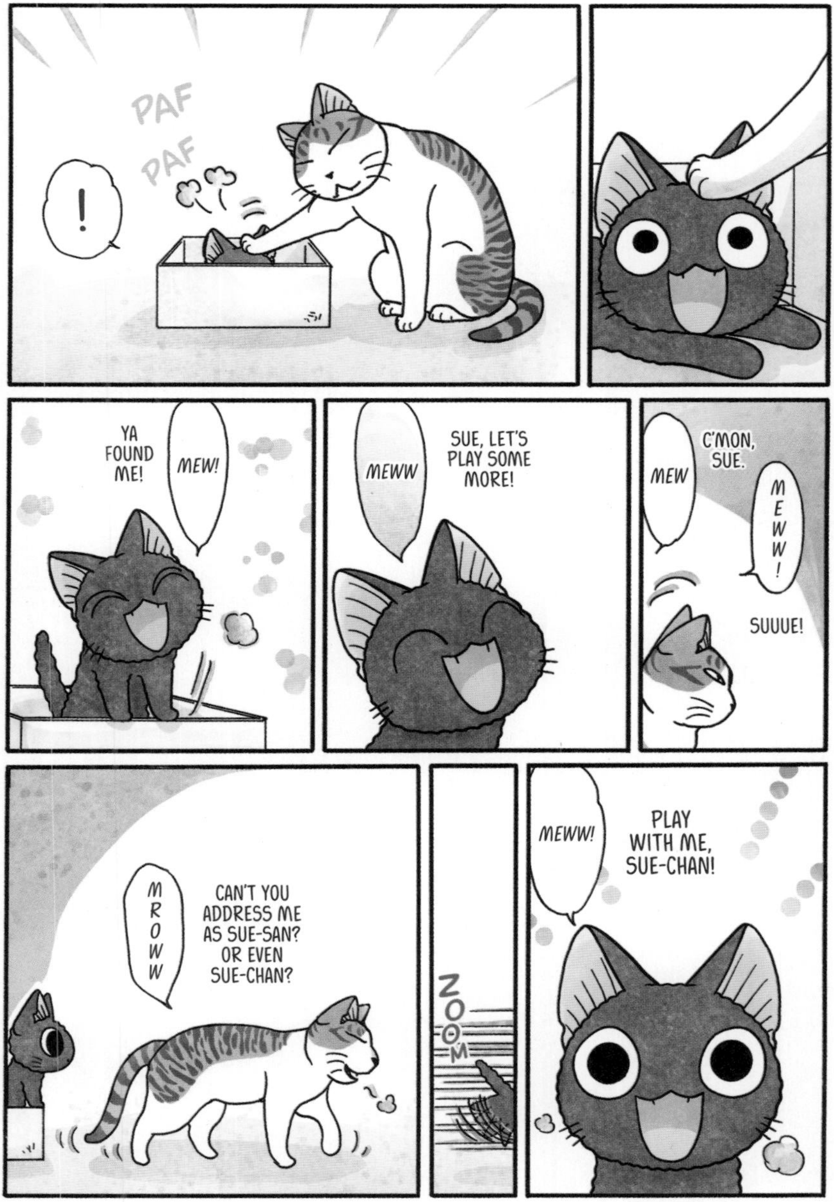
PAF
PAF
!
YA FOUND ME!
MEW!
MEWW
SUE, LET'S PLAY SOME MORE!
MEW
C'MON, SUE.
MEWW!
SUUUE!
MROWW
CAN'T YOU ADDRESS ME AS SUE-SAN? OR EVEN SUE-CHAN?
ZOOM
MEWW!
PLAY WITH ME, SUE-CHAN!

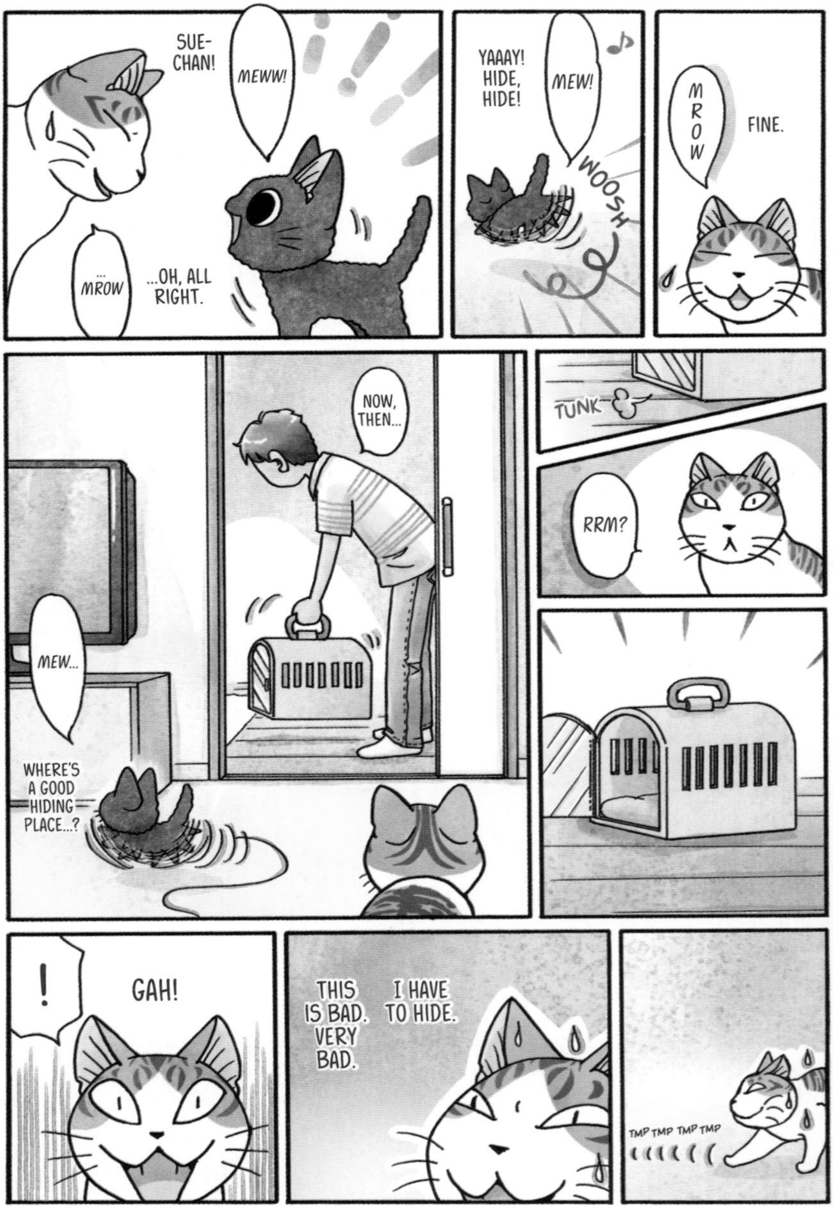

SUE-CHAN!
MEWW!
... MROW
...OH, ALL RIGHT.
YAAAY! HIDE, HIDE!
MEW!
WOOSH
MROW
FINE.
NOW, THEN...
MEW...
WHERE'S A GOOD HIDING PLACE...?
TUNK
RRM?
!
GAH!
THIS IS BAD. VERY BAD.
I HAVE TO HIDE.
TMP TMP TMP TMP

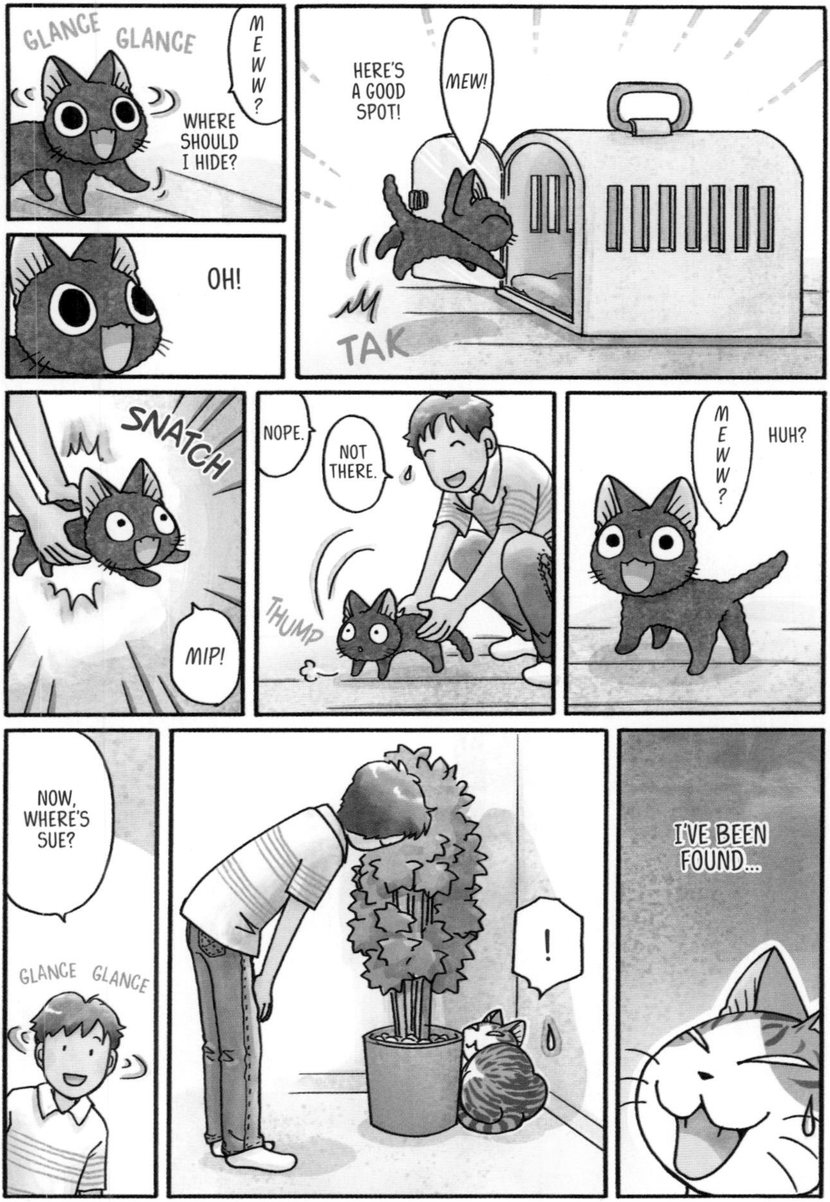
GLANCE GLANCE
MEWW?
WHERE SHOULD I HIDE?
OH!
HERE'S A GOOD SPOT!
MEW!
TAK
SNATCH
MIP!
NOPE.
NOT THERE.
THUMP
MEWW?
HUH?
NOW, WHERE'S SUE?
GLANCE GLANCE
!
I'VE BEEN FOUND...

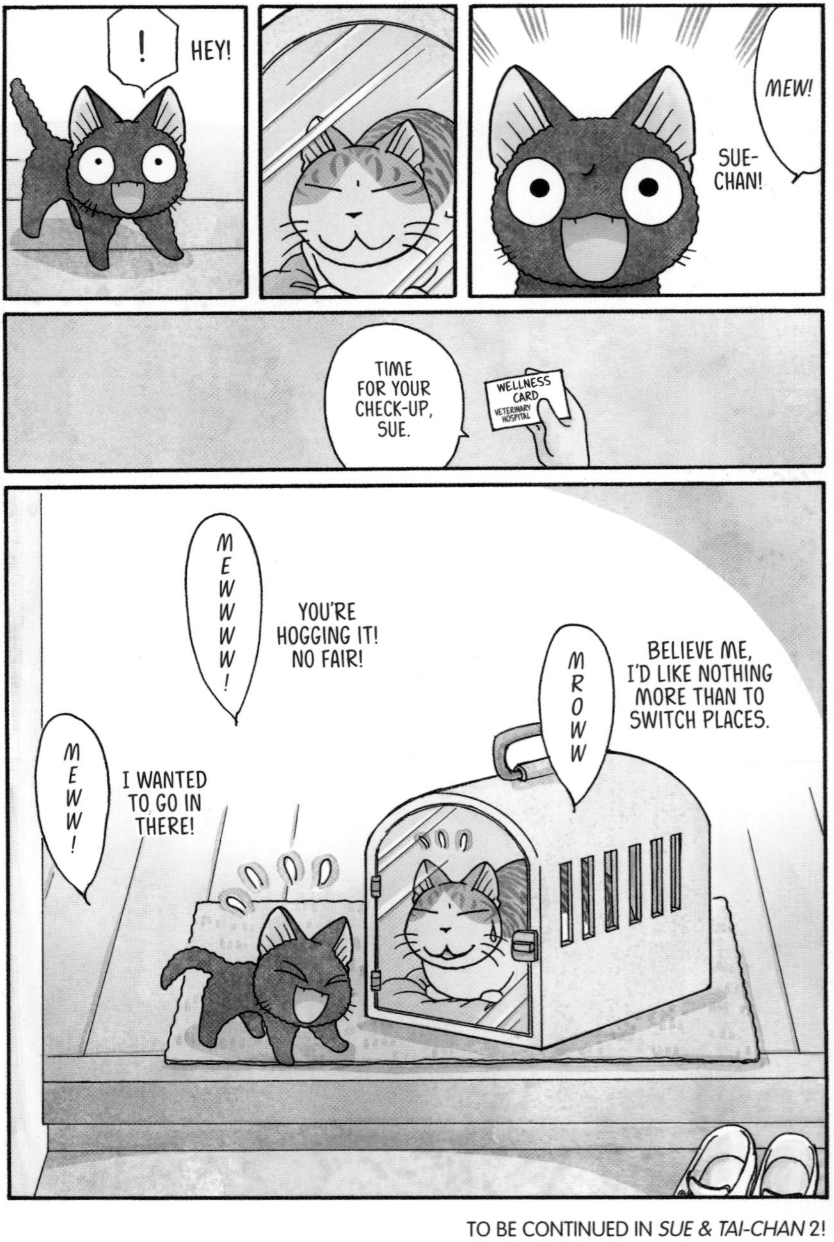
!
HEY!
MEW!
SUE-CHAN!
TIME FOR YOUR CHECK-UP, SUE.
WELLNESS CARD
VETERINARY HOSPITAL
MEWWWWW!
YOU'RE HOGGING IT! NO FAIR!
MROWW
BELIEVE ME, I'D LIKE NOTHING MORE THAN TO SWITCH PLACES.
MEWW!
I WANTED TO GO IN THERE!

TO BE CONTINUED IN *SUE & TAI-CHAN* 2!

WHAT'S THAT?

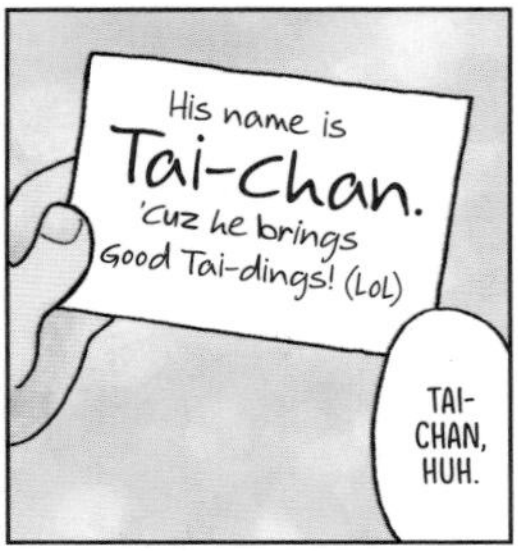

His name is
Tai-Chan.
'Cuz he brings
Good Tai-dings! (LoL)
TAI-CHAN, HUH.

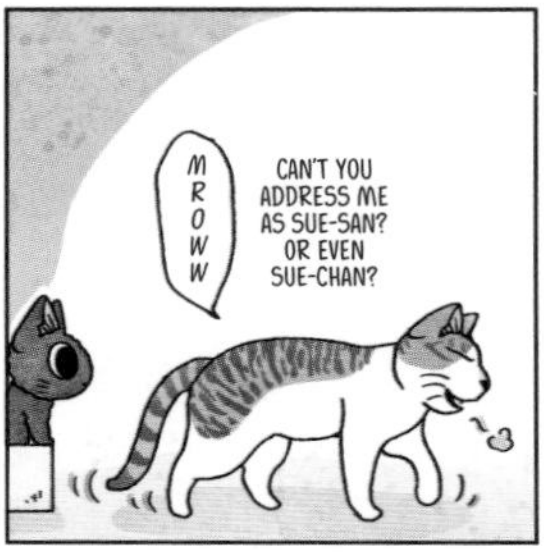

MROWW
CAN'T YOU ADDRESS ME AS SUE-SAN? OR EVEN SUE-CHAN?

In the Japanese language, there are words called "honorifics" that you can add after names to show how you feel toward that person or thing.

-chan is a cutesy honorific for showing affection, like for a close friend, a pet, or a young child. So, "Tai-chan" would be like saying "Little Tai."

-san is a polite honorific for showing respect, like "Mr.", "Ms.", or "Mx."

Not using an honorific means you must be *very* close to someone, so if you're not careful, it could be rude. Imagine calling your teacher by just their first name!

Sue & Tai-chan

FUKU FUKU

Kitten Tales

Konami Kanata

Craving More Cute Cat Comics?

Want to see more furry feline antics? A new series by Konami Kanata, author of the beloved *Chi's Sweet Home* series, tells the story of a tiny kitten named FukuFuku who lives with a kindly old lady. Each day brings something new to learn, the change of the seasons leads to exciting discoveries and even new objects to shred with freshly-grown claws.

Join FukuFuku and her charming owner on this quietly heartwarming journey of kittenhood.

Both Parts 1 and 2 On Sale Now!

This Book is the Cat's Meow

Celebrating the conclusion of Konami Kanata's international megahit *Chi's Sweet Home*, **The Complete Chi** is a new edition that honors some of the best Japan has ever offered in the field of cat comics. A multiple *New York Times* Best-Seller and two-time winner of the *Manga.Ask.com* Awards for Best Children's Manga, Konami Kanata's tale of a lost kitten has been acclaimed by readers worldwide as an excellent example of a comic that has truly been accepted by readers of all ages.

Presented in a brand new larger omnibus format each edition compiles three volumes of kitty cartoon tales, including two bonus cat comics from Konami Kanata's **FukuFuku** franchise, making **The Complete Chi's Sweet Home** a must have for every cat lover out there.

"Chi's Sweet Home made me smile throughout... It's utterly endearing. This is the first manga I've read in several years where I'm looking forward to the [next] volume."

—Chris Beveridge, *Mania.com*

"Konami Kanata does some pretty things with watercolor, and paces each of the little vignettes chronicling Chi's new life to highlight just the right moments for maximum effect... This is truly a visual treat."

—*Comics and More*

All Parts 1 - 4
Available Now!

The Complete
Chi's
Sweet Home

Konami Kanata

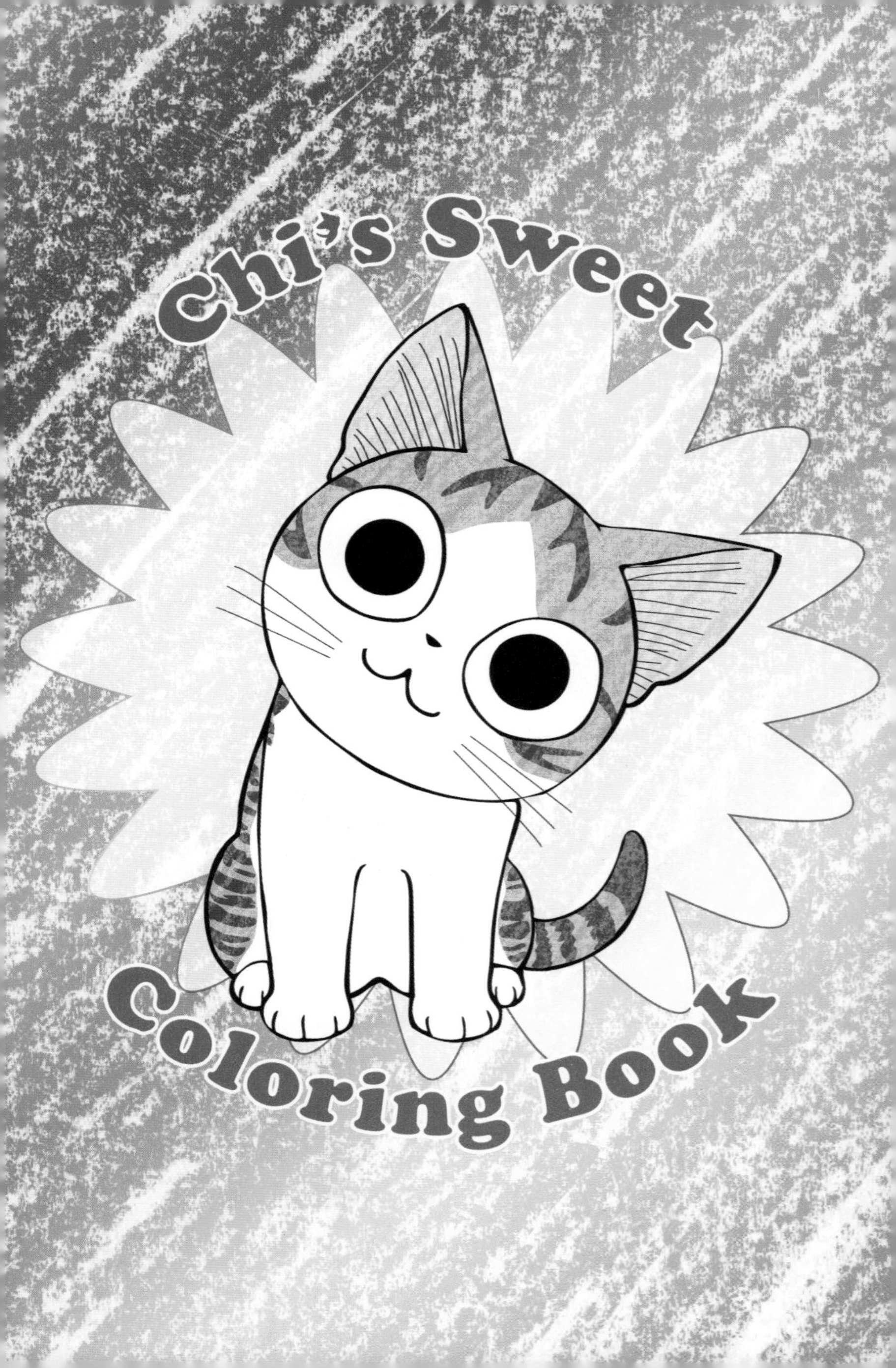
Chi's Sweet
Coloring Book

Chi returns to the US in a coloring book
featuring dozens of cute and furry illustrations from
award-winning cartoonist Konami Kanata.

On Sale Now!

Created by Konami Kanata
Adapted by Kinoko Natsume

Chi is back! Manga's most famous cat
returns with a brand new series!
Chi's Sweet Adventures collects dozens
of new full-color kitty tales made
for readers of all ages!

Volumes 1-4
On Sale Now!

Chi's

Sweet Adventures

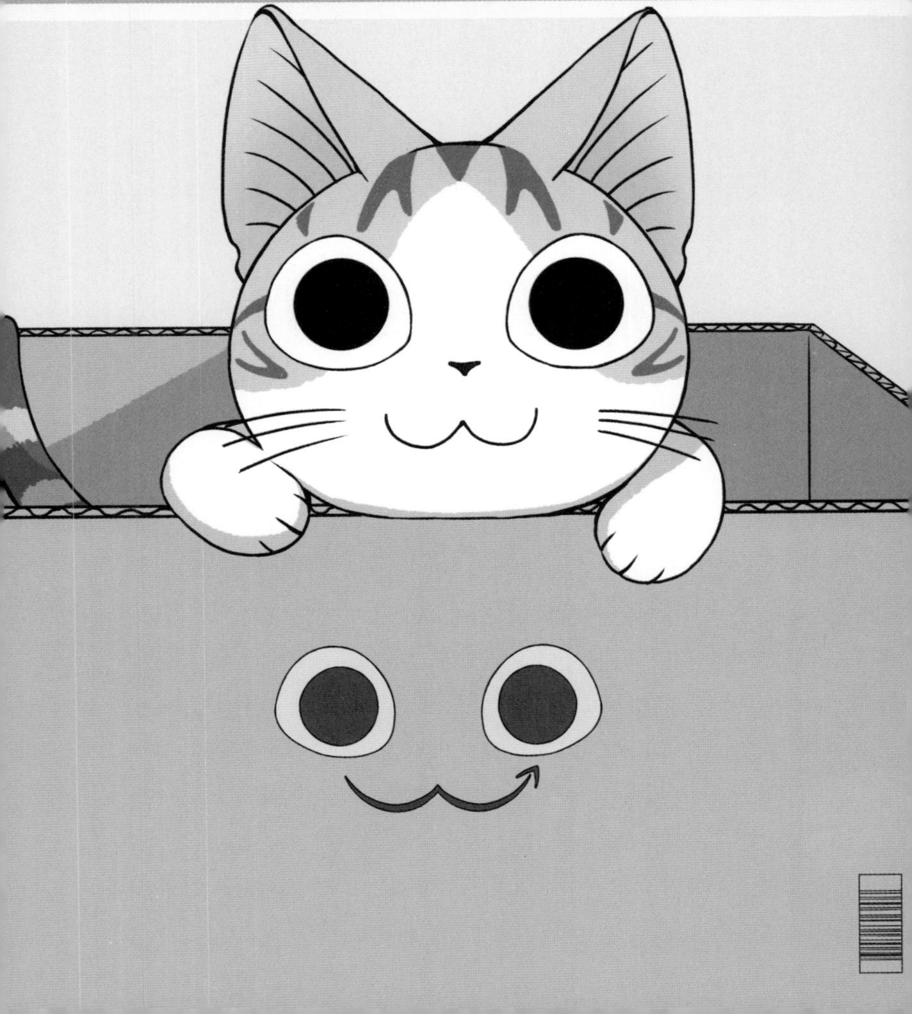

Next Volume

Tai-chan has settled in nicely into his life with Sue!

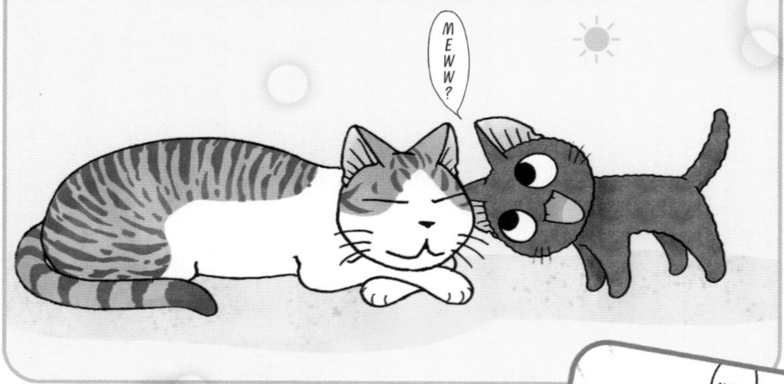
MEWW?

Maybe...

...a little TOO nicely?!

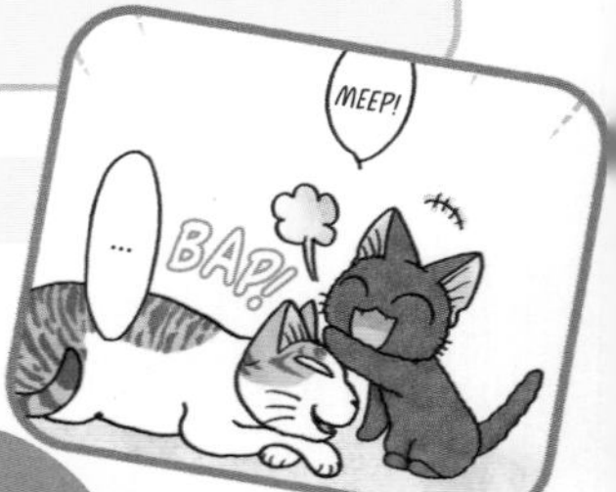
MEEP!
...
BAP!

Will the over-indulged kitten Tai-chan...

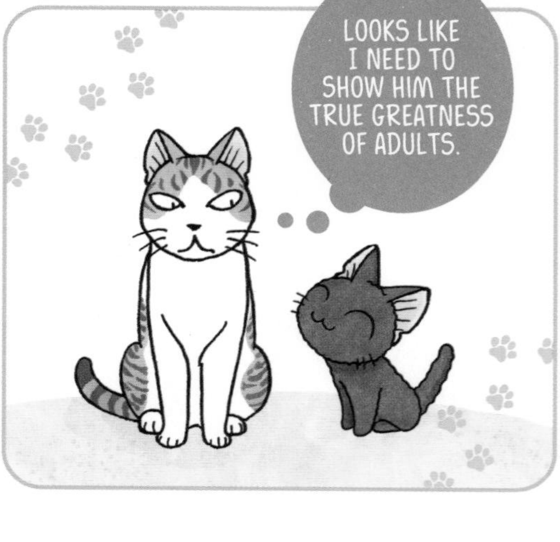
LOOKS LIKE I NEED TO SHOW HIM THE TRUE GREATNESS OF ADULTS.

...benefit from Sue's educational guidance?!

What's more...
There are lots of new feline faces to meet!!!

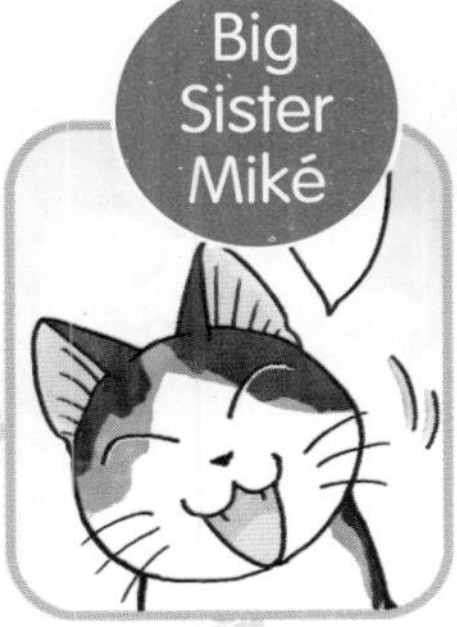
Big Sister Miké

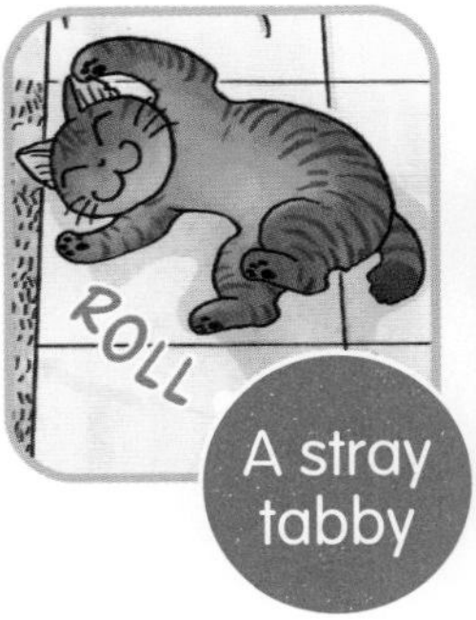
ROLL
A stray tabby

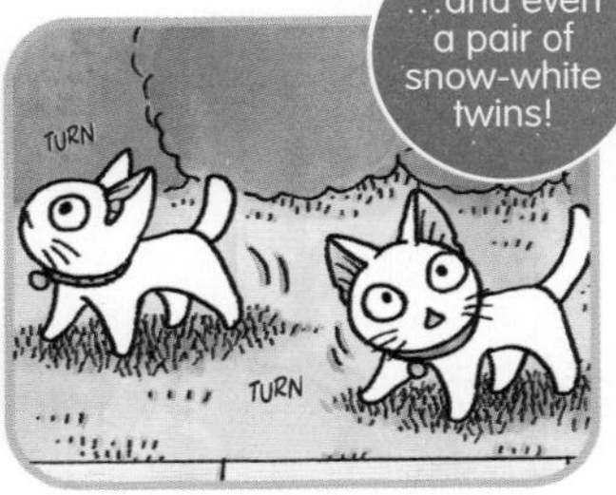
...and even a pair of snow-white twins!
TURN
TURN

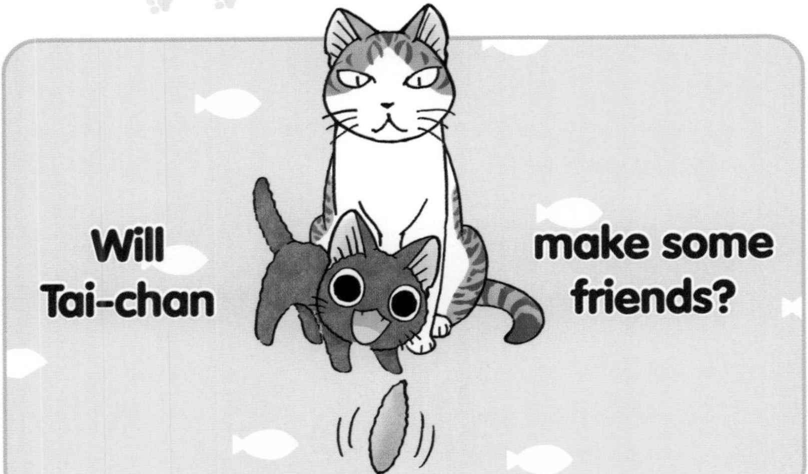
Will Tai-chan make some friends?

An old cat and a young cat—the oddest but cutest pair!

Sue & Tai-chan 2

A Kodansha Comics Trade Paperback Original
Sue & Tai-chan 1 copyright © 2017 Konami Kanata
English translation copyright © 2020 Konami Kanata

Published in the United States by Kodansha Comics, an imprint of Kodansha USA Publishing, LLC, New York.

Publication rights for this English edition arranged through Kodansha Ltd., Tokyo.

First published in Japan in 2017 by Kodansha Ltd., Tokyo.

ISBN 978-1-63236-939-0

Original cover design by Kohei Nawata Design Office

Printed in China

www.kodansha.us

9 8 7 6 5 4 3 2
Translation: Melissa Tanaka
Lettering: Phil Christie
Editing: Vanessa Tenazas
Kodansha Comics edition cover design by Phil Balsman

Publisher: Kiichiro Sugawara
Vice president of marketing & publicity: Naho Yamada

Director of publishing services: Ben Applegate
Associate director of operations: Stephen Pakula
Publishing services managing editor: Noelle Webster
Assistant production manager: Emi Lotto, Angela Zurlo
Logo and character art ©Kodansha USA Publishing, LLC